WORDSWORTH CLASSICS
OF WORLD LITERATURE

General Editor: Tom Griffith

THE SOCIAL CONTRACT

Jean-Jacques Rousseau
The Social Contract
or Principles of Political Right

❖

Translation by H. J. Tozer
Introduction by Derek Matravers

WORDSWORTH CLASSICS
OF WORLD LITERATURE

For my husband
ANTHONY JOHN RANSON
with love from your wife, the publisher.
Eternally grateful for your unconditional love,
not just for me but for our children,
Simon, Andrew and Nichola Trayler

4

Readers who are interested in other titles from
Wordsworth Editions are invited to visit our website at
www.wordsworth-editions.com

For our latest list and a full mail-order service contact
Bibliophile Books, 5 Thomas Road, London E14 7BN
TEL: +44 (0)20 7515 9222 FAX: +44 (0)20 7538 4115
E-MAIL: orders@bibliophilebooks.com

This edition published 1998 by Wordsworth Editions Limited
8B East Street, Ware, Hertfordshire SG12 9ET

ISBN 978-1-85326-781-9

Wordsworth® is a registered trademark of
Wordsworth Editions Limited,
the company founded by Michael Trayler in 1987

Typeset by Antony Gray
Printed and bound in Great Britain by
Clays Ltd, St Ives plc

CONTENTS

BOOK THREE

BOOK FOUR

INTRODUCTION

The Social Contract opens with the most quotable line in political philosophy: 'Man is born free, and everywhere he is in chains.' Slogans simplify, and this famous sentence unfortunately encourages a mistaken idea of the message of *The Social Contract*. It suggests that to be free, we must throw off the chains of civil society. In reality, *The Social Contract* says the opposite: it shows how we can live in the chains of society without compromising our freedom. It contains a theory of civil society which promises a free and equal relationship between the individual and the state. Its powerful message has been favoured by revolutionaries from Marat (who read it at street corners to incite the Paris mob) to Che Guevara (who apparently took it on campaigns, along with his Marx).

Jean-Jacques Rousseau was born in Geneva in 1712 and died in Paris in 1778. Apart from *The Social Contract*, two of his other works are still read widely: his fascinating autobiography, *The Confessions*, and his treatise on education, human nature and much else, *Emile*. Eighteenth-century France was, in general, an age in which intellectuals accepted that progress could be achieved by the application of reason to human affairs. Rousseau – a passionate Romantic – distrusted this. In most of his writing we find the voice of the living, feeling individual against the system. *The Social Contract* is the exception. It presents a positive view of how civil society would have to be in order to be acceptable and is, even now, radical in its implications. It was published, along with *Emile*, in 1762. The subsequent furore (the books were burned in Geneva) precipitated Rousseau's flight to England. It was read widely, and taken up by the Jacobins, one of the most extreme groups involved in the French Revolution (which began, after Rousseau's death, in 1789). At the height of 'the terror', Robespierre, the Jacobin leader, spoke in praise of Rousseau and had his ashes moved to the Panthéon. The question, how a work which seeks to preserve the freedom of each and every individual could be used to justify the terrorising of a civil population, is one to which I shall return below.

The Social Contract is divided into four books. The first considers the principles behind a just civil state, and is the most philosophically interesting. The second describes the state in more detail and lays down the relations between its elements. The third considers government and its various forms and the fourth considers ways in which the civil state can strengthen itself from the inside. It is not always easy to tell whether Rousseau is discussing principle or practicality, and as a result some of the claims made do not sit happily together. He seems aware of this, and at one stage (II, 5) plaintively remarks, 'All my ideas are connected, but I could not expound them all at once.' To get the most out of this book, in which there is a consistent line of argument, we have to take him at his word. The sympathetic reader will generally find a way through.

The question, for Rousseau, is whether the civil state can be so constituted that its members do not lose that which is their right by birth: namely, their freedom. In common with other political theorists, then and now, he contrasts the civil state with 'the state of nature'. The state of nature is the world in the absence of civil society. As a rough, intuitive picture we can think of it as a world of isolated hunter-gatherers. Rousseau is not making an historical claim, it does not matter whether he is correct in the details of what the world was actually like; it is a thought experiment. If we imagine what the world would be like in the absence of a civil society, we will be able to see the points of similarity and difference with the world organised into a civil society.

The problem is 'To find a form of association which may defend and protect with the whole force of the community the person and property of every associate, and by means of which each, coalescing with all, may nevertheless obey only himself, and remain as free as before. Such is the fundamental problem of which the social contract provides the solution.' (I, 6.) How can I live in a society, and be subject to all the laws current in that society, and yet be as free as I was in the state of nature? If I was hungry in the state of nature I had simply to pull some fruit off a tree. In a civil society I can only do that if it is my tree; if it is someone else's tree I will be punished for theft.

Rousseau's solution to this conundrum begins by separating various different 'wills' ('will' here is to be understood as 'desire'). An individual's particular will is that which is in his or her private and personal interest, which (naturally) tends only to his or her own advantage. The 'will of all' of a group is the aggregate of the particular wills of each of that group's members. The 'general will', Rousseau's greatest contribution to political thought, is the will which is in the best interests of the group considered as a whole. One instructive way to think about this is to imagine the group as a single individual. The general will is what such an individual would think, if it were thinking correctly and in its own best interest.

A simple example should make this clear. It is in the interests of each member of a sports team to be covered in glory – that is their particular will. The will of all is the sum of these: that they should all be covered in glory, be part of a winning team. The general will is what is in the best interests of the team: that it should win. Although the will of all and the general will are both that the team should win, they are quite different. The will of all is the pursuit of individual glory through the team winning, and the general will is simply that the team should win (even if this means players sacrificing their own glory, perhaps by volunteering for substitution).

There are difficulties in the claim that a group has an interest independent of the interests of all its members added together. To substantiate this, Rousseau has to imagine society as an organic whole into which each individual transfers his interest. This can just about be imagined if one considers the kind of small Swiss mountain state Rousseau knew and idolised. There are suggestions, in *The Social Contract*, of how this unity should be brought about: religion should serve social cohesion; there should be a censor to 'uphold morality', and, more worrying for modern liberal minds, discursive politics should be suppressed: 'The more that harmony reigns in the assemblies, that is, the more the voting approaches unanimity, the more also is the general will predominant; but long discussions, dissensions, and uproar proclaim the ascendancy of private interests and the decline of the state.' (IV, 2) The dangers in this will be considered below.

The problem is to make personal freedom and citizenship of a state compatible. This could be solved if it could be shown that what an individual wants and what society wants necessarily coincide. If, in matters fundamental to the state, the individual were to adopt the general will, then what the individual wants and what the state wants would be identical and there would be no loss of freedom.

This immediately prompts the question why an individual should want to adopt the general will. If their particular will is that which is in their best interests, considered as individuals, why not operate according to that? The answer, says Rousseau, is that it is only by obeying the general will that human beings can escape their animal, appetitive nature and achieve a moral standing. 'The passage from the state of nature to the civil state produces in man a very remarkable change, by substituting in his conduct justice for instinct, and by giving his actions the moral quality that they had previously lacked . . . Although, in this state, he is deprived of many advantages that he desires from nature, he acquires equally great ones in return; his faculties are exercised and developed; his ideas are expanded; his feelings are ennobled; his whole soul is exalted to such a degree that, if the abuses of this new condition did not often degrade him below that from which he has emerged, he ought to bless without ceasing the happy moment which released him from it for ever, and transformed him from a stupid and ignorant animal into an intelligent being and a man.' (I, 8.) There is an intimate link between our individual characters and the society in which we live. The move to civil society changes our characters for the better, and thus obeying the general will is a matter of obeying the worthy and worthwhile side of our nature.

What is at issue here is of central importance to political philosophy. In an earlier work, the *Discourse on Inequality*, Rousseau highlighted the erosion of the perfect freedom enjoyed in the state of nature by the onset of the civil state. This thought is preserved in *The Social Contract*; we lose the freedom to follow our inclinations. The new thought, however, is that this loss is small compared to the gain of real freedom – the freedom to operate within the benefits which emerge from the civil state. It is the difference between the opportunity to follow one's inclinations and the opportunity to form the inclinations suitable to one as 'an intelligent being and a man'. A modern example of the contrast is the difference between a drug addict's freedom from interference in taking the drug, and a greater freedom which would be freedom from that inclination.

Do we always need to act in conformity with the general will? And how do we come to know the general will? It is obvious, first, that the general will covers only matters in which our resulting actions will affect other people; which shirt I wear can (usually) be left to my particular will. However, it is unclear in Rousseau's text whether the general will should cover only utterly fundamental matters, such as the constitution of the state, or be broader than this. On balance, I think the text favours the latter interpretation. On the second question, we come to know the general will by taking a vote. Provided the vote is taken in circumstances of a rough equality of wealth and power, and individuals vote not on their particular wills but on what they take the general will to be, the majority view will reveal the general will. (This method of discovering truths was given a sound statistical basis by Condorcet twenty years later.) It is important to realise that, unlike a modern democracy in which the majority *constitutes* the will of the state, Rousseau uses voting as a method of *discovering* the view of the state.

In short, Rousseau thinks we can be both ruled and free only if we rule ourselves. We do this by thinking of ourselves as part of a common whole, and adopting the perspective of the whole. This is tied in closely with Rousseau's discussion of practical politics – in particular, the controversial figure of the legislator. Rousseau's problem is that we think of ourselves as part of a common whole only if we are members of a civil society, but will not become members of a civil society unless we think of ourselves as part of a whole. (II, 7.) The answer to this chicken-and-egg problem is the quasi-divine figure of the legislator who manages to instantiate the general will in a single person – although Rousseau was not hopeful that such a person could be found. Whatever one thinks of Rousseau's solution, the problem is real and not one which political theorists are keen to face.

The people are the sovereign body of the state; it is their general will which is the law. However, the people are a cumbersome instrument with which to enact the law and run a state effectively.

Hence a government is needed. The government is the servant of the people; it is there simply to enact the general will. It possesses no independent sovereign authority, and may be changed or abolished at the will of the people. Rousseau considers various forms of government: democracy, aristocracy and monarchy. Direct, participatory democracy is rejected; 'so perfect a government is unsuited to men.' (IV, 4.) This is not surprising, given Rousseau's literal reading of the term. In a democracy, the sovereign and the government have the same members: all the people in the state. A government of that scale would be utterly inefficient, except, once again, in the kind of small state Rousseau held as an ideal.

Rousseau's account proposes to preserve the freedom of each and every individual and maintain a free and equal relationship between individuals and the state. How, then, did it come to be used to justify the terror? How could Bertrand Russell write, as he did in 1946, that 'the dictatorships of Russia and Germany (especially the latter) are in part an outcome of Rousseau's teaching'? Critics have concentrated on two weaknesses in the account, both resulting from the contrast Rousseau draws between natural and civil freedom.

First, there is the problem that if the general will represents what the people *really* want, then forcing them to obey the general will, even if they think they want something else, helps them to be free rather than restricts their freedom. Breaking a drug addict's habit (even against their will) could be seen as increasing their freedom, but it is unattractive as a political ideal. Dictators through the centuries have justified repressing people by saying that they are enacting the real will of the people; the Soviet Union locked dissidents up in asylums on the grounds that anyone who opposed the system must be mad, rather than different or bad. Rousseau's idea of forcing people to be free follows quite naturally from thinking that people can be mistaken about their 'real' interests, but it can be – indeed, has been – politically disastrous.

Second, the drive to realise the general will means, as we have seen, that Rousseau denies the legitimacy of, and would ban, all private associations. Again, this follows from his desire to have the people vote from the perspective of the whole, rather than from any individual or group perspective. This seems, to a modern liberal, intolerant and manipulative. Given that the only group Rousseau would allow is a civil religion to cultivate the moral personalities of the citizens, we must suspect that Rousseau's society requires too much homogeneity and is too intolerant of difference.

Rousseau's vision of a free society as one that is governed by its members is an attractive one. However, if we doubt that there is a single answer to what is best for a society, that is, if we doubt that there is a perspective of the whole, a general will, then our vision of a society that governs itself becomes very different. Where Rousseau desired homogeneity and unanimity to ensure access to an independently given general will, we value discord and debate (and thus the flourishing of different groups). The difference is that we see what is best for society as *constructed* by politics and debate, whereas Rousseau thought it merely discovered by such practices.

In abandoning the general will, we abandon the core of Rousseau's account. There are three important reasons, however, why we should continue to read *The Social Contract*. The first is that it is one of the few great defences of the civil society. Questions of the legitimacy of government, and how to get people to obey rules that are not in their interest, are still with us. It is salutary to bear in mind that while Rousseau might have respected our efforts to locate sovereignty with the people, he would have criticised the apparent failure of majoritarian conceptions of democracy to ensure representation of minority views (look back at his fundamental problem: '*each* . . . may nevertheless obey only himself'). The second reason is its profound importance in the history of political theory. This is not limited to its use (or misuse) by French and American revolutionaries, but extends to its influence on subsequent thought. Kant's moral theory has some close affinities with the general will (an etching of Rousseau was the only picture to adorn Kant's house), and some aspects of Marx's theory (particularly his discussions of alienation) are similar to ideas which received sustained examination by Rousseau. However, the best argument for reading it is in the book itself; *The Social Contract* is a passionate and idealistic working out of a theory of the civil state which would enable us to develop not only as citizens of a state, but as free beings and moral equals.

DEREK MATRAVERS
The Open University

SUGGESTIONS FOR FURTHER READING

I. Berlin, 'Two Concepts of Liberty', in his *Four Essays on Liberty*, Oxford University Press, 1969

N. Dent, *A Rousseau Dictionary*, Blackwell, 1992

I. Hampsher-Monk, 'Rousseau', in his *A History of Modern Political Thought*, Blackwell, 1992

T. Hobbes, *Leviathan*

J. Locke, *An Essay Concerning the True Original, Extent and End of Civil Government*

J. S. Mill, *On Liberty*

T. Paine, *Rights of Man*

J-J. Rousseau, *The Confessions*

J. Wolff, *An Introduction to Political Philosophy*, Oxford University Press, 1996

THE SOCIAL CONTRACT

PREFATORY NOTE

This little treatise is extracted from a larger work undertaken at an earlier time without consideration of my capacity, and long since abandoned. Of the various fragments that might be selected from what was accomplished, the following is the most considerable, and appears to me the least unworthy of being offered to the public. The rest of the work is no longer in existence.

INTRODUCTORY NOTE

I wish to enquire whether, taking men as they are and laws as they can be made, it is possible to establish some just and certain rule of administration in civil affairs. In this investigation I shall always strive to reconcile what right permits with what interest prescribes, so that justice and utility may not be severed.

I enter upon this enquiry without demonstrating the importance of my subject. I shall be asked whether I am a prince or a legislator that I write on politics. I reply that I am not; and that it is for this very reason that I write on politics. If I were a prince or a legislator, I should not waste my time in saying what ought to be done; I should do it or remain silent.

Having been born a citizen of a free state, and a member of the sovereign body, however feeble an influence my voice may have in public affairs, the right to vote upon them is sufficient to impose on me the duty of informing myself about them; and I feel happy, whenever I meditate on governments, always to discover in my researches new reasons for loving that of my own country.

BOOK ONE

CHAPTER 1

Subject of the First Book

Man is born free, and everywhere he is in chains. Many a one believes himself the master of others, and yet he is a greater slave than they. How has this change come about? I do not know. What can render it legitimate? I believe that I can settle this question.

If I considered only force and the results that proceed from it, I should say that so long as a people is compelled to obey and does obey, it does well; but that, so soon as it can shake off the yoke and does shake it off, it does better; for, if men recover their freedom by virtue of the same right by which it was taken away, either they are justified in resuming it, or there was no justification for depriving them of it. But the social order is a sacred right which serves as a foundation for all others. This right, however, does not come from nature. It is therefore based on conventions. The question is to know what these conventions are. Before coming to that, I must establish what I have just laid down.

CHAPTER 2

Primitive Societies

The earliest of all societies, and the only natural one, is the family; yet children remain attached to their father only so long as they have need of him for their own preservation. As soon as this need ceases, the natural bond is dissolved. The children being freed from the obedience which they owed to their father, and the father from the cares which he owed to his children, become equally independent. If they remain united, it is no longer naturally but voluntarily; and the family itself is kept together only by convention.

This common liberty is a consequence of man's nature. His first law is to attend to his own preservation, his first cares are those which he owes to himself; and as soon as he comes to years of discretion, being sole judge of the means adapted for his own preservation, he becomes his own master.

The family is, then, if you will, the primitive model of political societies; the chief is the analogue of the father, while the people represent the children; and all, being born free and equal, alienate their liberty only for their own advantage. The whole difference is that, in the family, the father's love for his children repays him for the care that he bestow; upon thems while, in the state, the pleasure of ruling makes up for the chief's lack of love for his people.

Grotius denies that all human authority is established for the benefit of the governed, and he cites slavery as an instance. His invariable mode of reasoning is to establish right by fact.* A juster

* 'Learned researches in public law are often nothing but the history of ancient abuses; and to devote much labour to studying them is misplaced pertinacity' (*Treatise on the Interests of France in Relation to her Neighbours*, by the Marquis d'Argenson). That is exactly what Grotius did.

method might be employed, but none more favourable to tyrants.

It is doubtful, then, according to Grotius, whether the human race belongs to a hundred men, or whether these hundred men belong to the human race; and he appears throughout his book to incline to the former opinion, which is also that of Hobbes. In this way we have mankind divided like herds of cattle, each of which has a master, who looks after it in order to devour it.

Just as a herdsman is superior in nature to his herd, so chiefs, who are the herdsmen of men, are superior in nature to their people. Thus, according to Philo's account, the Emperor Caligula reasoned, inferring truly enough from this analogy that kings are gods, or that men are brutes.

The reasoning of Caligula is tantamount to that of Hobbes and Grotius. Aristotle, before them all, had likewise said that men are not naturally equal, but that some are born for slavery and others for dominion.

Aristotle was right but he mistook the effect for the cause. Every man born in slavery is born for slavery; nothing is more certain. Slaves lose everything in their bonds, even the desire to escape from them; they love their servitude as the companions of Ulysses loved their brutishness.* If, then, there are slaves by nature, it is because there have been slaves contrary to nature. The first slaves were made such by force; their cowardice kept them in bondage.

I have said nothing about King Adam nor about Emperor Noah, the father of three great monarchs who shared the universe, like the children of Saturn with whom they are supposed to be identical. I hope that my moderation will give satisfaction; for, as I am a direct descendant of one of these princes, and perhaps of the eldest branch, how do I know whether, by examination of titles, I might not find myself the lawful king of the human race? Be that as it may, it cannot be denied that Adam was sovereign of the world, as Robinson was of his island, so long as he was its sole inhabitant; and it was an agreeable feature of that empire that the monarch, secure on his throne, had nothing to fear from rebellions, or wars, or conspirators.

* See a small treatise by Plutarch, entitled *That Brutes Employ Reason*.

CHAPTER 3

The Right of the Strongest

The strongest man is never strong enough to be always master, unless he transforms his power into right, and obedience into duty. Hence the right of the strongest — a right apparently assumed in irony, and really established in principle. But will this phrase never be explained to us? Force is a physical power; I do not see what morality can result from its effects. To yield to force is an act of necessity, not of will; it is at most an act of prudence. In what sense can it be a duty?

Let us assume for a moment this pretended right. I say that nothing results from it but inexplicable nonsense; for if force constitutes right, the effect changes with the cause, and any force which overcomes the first succeeds to its rights. As soon as men can disobey with impunity, they may do so legitimately; and since the strongest is always in the right, the only thing is to act in such a way that one may be the strongest. But what sort of a right is it that perishes when force ceases? If it is necessary to obey by compulsion, there is no need to obey from duty; and if men are no longer forced to obey, obligation is at an end. We see, then, that this word *right* adds nothing to force; it here means nothing at all.

Obey the powers that be. If that means, yield to force, the precept is good but superfluous; I reply that it will never be violated. All power comes from God, I admit; but every disease comes from him too; does it follow that we are prohibited from calling in a physician? If a brigand should surprise me in the recesses of a wood, am I bound not only to give up my purse when forced, but am I also morally bound to do so when I might conceal it? For, in effect, the pistol which he holds is a superior force.

Let us agree, then, that might does not make right, and that we are bound to obey none but lawful authorities. Thus my original question ever recurs.

CHAPTER 4

Slavery

Since no man has any natural authority over his fellow men, and since force is not the source of right, conventions remain as the basis of all lawful authority among men.

If an individual, says Grotius, can alienate his liberty and become the slave of a master, why should not a whole people be able to alienate theirs, and become subject to a king? In this there are many equivocal terms requiring explanation; but let us confine ourselves to the word *alienate*. To alienate is to give or sell. Now, a man who becomes another's slave does not give himself; he sells himself at the very least for his subsistence. But why does a nation sell itself? So far from a king supplying his subjects with their subsistence, he draws his from them; and, according to Rabelais, a king does not live on a little. Do subjects, then, give up their persons on condition that their property also shall be taken? I do not see what is left for them to keep.

It will be said that the despot secures to his subjects civil peace. Be it so; but what do they gain by that, if the wars which his ambition brings upon them, together with his insatiable greed and the vexations of his administration, harass them more than their own dissensions would? What do they gain by it if this tranquillity is itself one of their miseries? Men live tranquilly also in dungeons; is that enough to make them contented there? The Greeks confined in the cave of the Cyclops lived peacefully until their turn came to be devoured.

To say that a man gives himself for nothing is to say what is absurd and inconceivable; such an act is illegitimate and invalid, for the simple reason that he who performs it is not in his right mind. To say the same thing of a whole nation is to suppose a nation of fools; and madness does not confer rights.

Even if each person could alienate himself, he could not alienate his children; they are born free men; their liberty belongs to them, and no one has a right to dispose of it except themselves. Before they have come to years of discretion, the father can, in their name, stipulate conditions for their preservation and welfare, but not surrender them irrevocably and unconditionally; for such a gift is contrary to the ends of nature, and exceeds the rights of paternity. In order, then, that an arbitrary government might be legitimate, it would be necessary that the people in each generation should have the option of accepting or rejecting it; but in that case such a government would no longer be arbitrary.

To renounce one's liberty is to renounce one's quality as a man, the rights and also the duties of humanity. For him who renounces everything there is no possible compensation. Such a renunciation is incompatible with man's nature, for to take away ail freedom from his will is to take away all morality from his actions. In short, a convention which stipulates absolute authority on the one side and unlimited obedience on the other is vain and contradictory. Is it not clear that we are under no obligations whatsoever towards a man from whom we have a right to demand everything? And does not this single condition, without equivalent, without exchange, involve the nullity of the act? For what right would my slave have against me since all that he has belongs to me? His rights being mine, this right of me against myself is a meaningless phrase.

Grotius and others derive from war another origin for the pretended right of slavery. The victor having, according to them, the right of slaying the vanquished, the latter may purchase his life at the cost of his freedom; an agreement so much the more legitimate that it turns to the advantage of both.

But it is manifest that this pretended right of slaying the vanquished in no way results from the state of war. Men are not naturally enemies, if only for the reason that, living in their primitive independence, they have no mutual relations sufficiently durable to constitute a state of peace or a state of war. It is the relation of things and not of men which constitutes war; and since the state of war cannot arise from simple personal relations, but only from real relations, private war – war between man and man – cannot exist either in the state of nature, where there is no settled ownership, or in the social state, where everything is under the authority of the laws.

Private combats, duels, and encounters are acts which do not constitute a state of war; and with regard to the private wars authorised by the Establishments of Louis IX, king of France, and suspended by the Peace of God, they were abuses of the feudal government, an absurd system if ever there was one, contrary both to the principles of natural right and to all sound government.

War, then, is not a relation between man and man, but a relation between state and state, in which individuals are enemies only by accident, not as men, nor even as citizens,* but as soldiers; not as members of the fatherland, but as its defenders. In short, each state can have as enemies only other states and not individual men, inasmuch as it is impossible to fix any true relation between things of different kinds.

This principle is also conformable to the established maxims of all ages and to the invariable practice of all civilised nations. Declarations of war are not so much warnings to the powers as to their subjects. The foreigner, whether king, or nation, or private person, that robs, slays, or detains subjects without declaring war against the government, is not an enemy, but a brigand. Even in open war, a just prince, while he rightly takes possession of all that belongs to the state in an enemy's country, respects the person and property of individuals; he respects the rights on which his own are based. The aim of war being the destruction of the hostile state, we have a

---

* The Romans, who understood and respected the rights of war better than any nation in the world, carried their scruples so far in this respect that no citizen was allowed to serve as a volunteer without enlisting expressly against the enemy, and by name against a certain enemy. A legion in which Cato the younger made his first campaign under Popilius having been re-formed, Cato the elder wrote to Popilius that, if he consented to his son's continuing to serve under him, it was necessary that he should take a new military oath, because, the first being annulled, he could no longer bear arms against the enemy (Cicero, *De Officiis* i, 11). And Cato also wrote to his son to abstain from appearing in battle until he had taken this new oath. I know that it will be possible to urge against me the siege of Clusium and other particular cases; but I cite laws and customs (Livy, v, 35–37). No nation has transgressed its laws less frequently than the Romans and no nation has had laws so admirable.

right to slay its defenders so long as they have arms in their hands; but as soon as they lay them down and surrender, ceasing to be enemies or instruments of the enemy, they become again simply men, and no one has any further right over their lives. Sometimes it is possible to destroy the state without killing a single one of its members; but war confers no right except what is necessary to its end. These are not the principles of Grotius; they are not based on the authority of poets, but are derived from the nature of things, and are founded on reason.

With regard to the right of conquest, it has no other foundation than the law of the strongest. If war does not confer on the victor the right of slaying the vanquished, this right, which he does not possess, cannot be the foundation of a right to enslave them. If we have a right to slay an enemy only when it is impossible to enslave him, the right to enslave him is not derived from the right to kill him; it is, therefore, an iniquitous bargain to make him purchase his life, over which the victor has no right, at the cost of his liberty. In establishing the right of life and death upon the right of slavery, and the right of slavery upon the right of life and death, is it not manifest that one falls into a vicious circle?

Even if we grant this terrible right of killing everybody, I say that a slave made in war, or a conquered nation, is under no obligation at all to a master, except to obey him so far as compelled. In taking an equivalent for his life the victor has conferred no favour on the slave; instead of killing him unprofitably, he has destroyed him for his own advantage. Far, then, from having acquired over him any authority in addition to that of force, the state of war subsists between them as before, their relation even is the effect of it; and the exercise of the rights of war supposes that there is no treaty of peace. They have made a convention. Be it so; but this convention, far from terminating the state of war, supposes its continuance.

Thus, in whatever way we regard things, the right of slavery is invalid, not only because it is illegitimate, but because it is absurd and meaningless. These terms, *slavery* and *right*, are contradictory and mutually exclusive. Whether addressed by a man to a man, or by a man to a nation, such a speech as this will always be equally foolish: 'I make an agreement with you wholly at your expense and wholly for my benefit, and I shall observe it as long as I please, while you also shall observe it as long as I please.'

CHAPTER 5

That it is Always Necessary to go Back to a First Convention

If I should concede all that I have so far refuted, those who favour despotism would be no farther advanced. There will always be a great difference between subduing a multitude and ruling a society. When isolated men, however numerous they may be, are subjected one after another to a single person, this seems to me only a case of master and slaves, not of a nation and its chief; they form, if you will, an aggregation, but not an association, for they have neither public property nor a body politic. Such a man, had he enslaved half the world, is never anything but an individual; his interest, separated from that of the rest, is never anything but a private interest. If he dies, his empire after him is left disconnected and disunited, as an oak dissolves and becomes a heap of ashes after the fire has consumed it.

A nation, says Grotius, can give itself to a king. According to Grotius, then, a nation is a nation before it gives itself to a king. This gift itself is a civil act, and presupposes a public resolution. Consequently, before examining the act by which a nation elects a king, it would be proper to examine the act by which a nation becomes a nation; for this act, being necessarily anterior to the other, is the real foundation of the society.

In fact, if there were no anterior convention, where, unless the election were unanimous, would be the obligation upon the minority to submit to the decision of the majority? And whence do the hundred who desire a master derive the right to vote on behalf of ten who do not desire one? The law of the plurality of votes is itself established by convention, and presupposes unanimity once at least.

CHAPTER 6

The Social Pact

I assume that men have reached a point at which the obstacles that endanger their preservation in the state of nature overcome, by their resistance, the forces which each individual can exert with a view to maintaining himself in that state. Then this primitive condition can no longer subsist, and the human race would perish unless it changed its mode of existence.

Now, as men cannot create any new forces, but only combine and direct those that exist, they have no other means of self-preservation than to form by aggregation a sum of forces which may overcome the resistance, to put them in action by a single motive power, and to make them work in concert.

This sum of forces can be produced only by the combination of many; but the strength and freedom of each man being the chief instruments of his preservation, how can he pledge them without injuring himself, and without neglecting the cares which he owes to himself? This difficulty, applied to my subject, may be expressed in these terms:

'To find a form of association which may defend and protect with the whole force of the community the person and property of every associate, and by means of which each, coalescing with all, may nevertheless obey only himself, and remain as free as before.' Such is the fundamental problem of which the social contract furnishes the solution.

The clauses of this contract are so determined by the nature of the act that the slightest modification would render them vain and ineffectual; so that, although they have never perhaps been formally enunciated, they are everywhere the same, everywhere tacitly admitted and recognised, until, the social pact being violated, each man regains his original rights and recovers his natural liberty, whilst losing the conventional liberty for which he renounced it.

These clauses, rightly understood, are reducible to one only, *viz.* the total alienation to the whole community of each associate with all his rights; for, in the first place, since each gives himself up entirely, the conditions are equal for all; and, the conditions being equal for all, no one has any interest in making them burdensome to others.

Further, the alienation being made without reserve, the union is as perfect as it can be, and an individual associate can no longer claim anything; for, if any rights were left to individuals, since there would be no common superior who could judge between them and the public, each, being on some point his own judge, would soon claim to be so on all; the state of nature would still subsist, and the association would necessarily become tyrannical or useless.

In short, each giving himself to all, gives himself to nobody; and as there is not one associate over whom we do not acquire the same rights which we concede to him over ourselves, we gain the equivalent of all that we lose, and more power to preserve what we have.

If, then, we set aside what is not of the essence of the social contract, we shall find that it is reducible to the following terms: 'Each of us puts in common his person and his whole power under the supreme direction of the general will; and in return we receive every member as an indivisible part of the whole.'

Forthwith, instead of the individual personalities of all the contracting parties, this act of association produces a moral and collective body, which is composed of as many members as the assembly has voices, and which receives from this same act its unity, its common self (*moi*), its life, and its will. This public person, which is thus formed by the union of all the individual members, formerly took the name of *city*,* and now takes that of

---

* The real meaning of this word has been almost completely effaced among the moderns; the majority take a town for a city, and a burgess for a citizen. They do not know that houses make the town, and that citizens make the city. This very mistake cost the Carthaginians dear. I have never read of the title citizens (*cives*) being given to the subjects of a prince, not even in ancient times to the Macedonians, nor, in our days, to the English, although nearer liberty than all the rest. The French alone employ familiarly this name *citizen*,

republic or *body politic*, which is called by its members *state* when it is passive, *sovereign* when it is active, *power* when it is compared to similar bodies. With regard to the associates, they take collectively the name of *people*, and are called individually *citizens*, as participating in the sovereign power, and *subjects*, as subjected to the laws of the state. But these terms are often confused and are mistaken one for another; it is sufficient to know how to distinguish them when they are used with complete precision.

---

because they have no true idea of it, as we can see from their dictionaries; but for this fact, they would, by assuming it, commit the crime of high treason. The name, among them, expresses a virtue, not a right. When Bodin wanted to give an account of our citizens and burgesses he made a gross blunder, mistaking the one for the other. M. d'Alembert has not erred in this, and, in his article *Geneva*, has clearly distinguished the four orders of men (even five, counting mere foreigners) which exist in our town, and of which two only compose the republic. No other French author that I know of has understood the real meaning of the word *citizen*.

CHAPTER 7

The Sovereign

We see from this formula that the act of association contains a reciprocal engagement between the public and individuals, and that every individual, contracting so to speak with himself, is engaged in a double relation, *viz*. as a member of the sovereign towards individuals, and as a member of the state towards the sovereign. But we cannot apply here the maxim of civil law that no one is bound by engagements made with himself; for there is a great difference between being bound to oneself and to a whole of which one forms part.

We must further observe that the public resolution which can bind all subjects to the sovereign in consequence of the two different relations under which each of them is regarded cannot, for a contrary reason, bind the sovereign to itself; and that accordingly it is contrary to the nature of the body politic for the sovereign to impose on itself a law which it cannot transgress. As it can only be considered under one and the same relation, it is in the position of an individual contracting with himself; whence we see that there is not, nor can be, any kind of fundamental law binding upon the body of the people, not even the social contract. This does not imply that such a body cannot perfectly well enter into engagements with others in what does not derogate from this contract; for, with regard to foreigners, it becomes a simple being, an individual.

But the body politic or sovereign, deriving its existence only from the sanctity of the contract, can never bind itself, even to others, in anything that derogates from the original act, such as alienation of some portion of itself, or submission to another sovereign. To violate the act by which it exists would be to annihilate itself; and what is nothing produces nothing.

So soon as the multitude is thus united in one body, it is

impossible to injure one of the members without attacking the body, still less to injure the body without the members feeling the effects. Thus duty and interest alike oblige the two contracting parties to give mutual assistance; and the men themselves should seek to combine in this twofold relationship all the advantages which are attendant on it.

Now, the sovereign, being formed only of the individuals that compose it, neither has nor can have any interest contrary to theirs; consequently the sovereign power needs no guarantee towards its subjects, because it is impossible that the body should wish to injure all its members; and we shall see hereafter that it can injure no one as an individual. The sovereign, for the simple reason that it is so, is always everything that it ought to be.

But this is not the case as regards the relation of subjects to the sovereign, which, notwithstanding the common interest, would have no security for the performance of their engagements, unless it found means to ensure their fidelity.

Indeed, every individual may, as a man, have a particular will contrary to, or divergent from, the general will which he has as a citizen; his private interest may prompt him quite differently from the common interest; his absolute and naturally independent existence may make him regard what he owes to the common cause as a gratuitous contribution, the loss of which will be less harmful to others than the payment of it will be burdensome to him; and, regarding the moral person that constitutes the state as an imaginary being because it is not a man, he would be willing to enjoy the rights of a citizen without being willing to fulfil the duties of a subject. The progress of such injustice would bring about the ruin of the body politic.

In order, then, that the social pact may not be a vain formulary, it tacitly includes this engagement, which can alone give force to the others, – that whoever refuses to obey the general will shall be constrained to do so by the whole body; which means nothing else than that he shall be forced to be free; for such is the condition which, uniting every citizen to his native land, guarantees him from all personal dependence, a condition that ensures the control and working of the political machine, and alone renders legitimate civil engagements, which, without it, would be absurd and tyrannical, and subject to the most enormous abuses.

CHAPTER 8

The Civil State

The passage from the state of nature to the civil state produces in man a very remarkable change, by substituting in his conduct justice for instinct, and by giving his actions the moral quality that they previously lacked. It is only when the voice of duty succeeds physical impulse, and law succeeds appetite, that man, who till then had regarded only himself, sees that he is obliged to act on other principles, and to consult his reason before listening to his inclinations. Although, in this state, he is deprived of many advantages that he derives from nature, he acquires equally great ones in return; his faculties are exercised and developed; his ideas are expanded; his feelings are ennobled; his whole soul is exalted to such a degree that, if the abuses of this new condition did not often degrade him below that from which he has emerged, he ought to bless without ceasing the happy moment that released him from it for ever, and transformed him from a stupid and ignorant animal into an intelligent being and a man.

Let us reduce this whole balance to terms easy to compare. What man loses by the social contract is his natural liberty and an unlimited right to anything which tempts him and which he is able to attain; what he gains is civil liberty and property in all that he possesses. In order that we may not be mistaken about these compensations, we must clearly distinguish natural liberty, which is limited only by the powers of the individual, from civil liberty, which is limited by the general will; and possession, which is nothing but the result of force or the right of first occupancy, from property, which can be based only on a positive title.

Besides the preceding, we might add to the acquisitions of the civil state moral freedom, which alone renders man truly master of himself; for the impulse of mere appetite is slavery, while obedience to a self-prescribed law is liberty. But I have already said too much on this head, and the philosophical meaning of the term *liberty* does not belong to my present subject.

CHAPTER 9

Real Property

Every member of the community at the moment of its formation gives himself up to it, just as he actually is, himself and all his powers, of which the property that he possesses forms part. By this act, possession does not change its nature when it changes hands, and become property in those of the sovereign; but, as the powers of the state (*cité*) are incomparably greater than those of an individual, public possession is also, in fact, more secure and more irrevocable, without being more legitimate, at least in respect of foreigners; for the state, with regard to its members, is owner of all their property by the social contract, which, in the state, serves as the basis of all rights; but with regard to other powers, it is owner only by the right of first occupancy which it derives from individuals.

The right of first occupancy, although more real than that of the strongest, becomes a true right only after the establishment of that of property. Every man has by nature a right to all that is necessary to him; but the positive act which makes him proprietor of certain property excludes him from all the residue. His portion having been allotted, he ought to confine himself to it, and he has no further right to the undivided property. That is why the right of first occupancy, so weak in the state of nature, is respected by every member of a state. In this right men regard not so much what belongs to others as what does not belong to themselves.

In order to legalise the right of first occupancy over any domain whatsoever, the following conditions are, in general, necessary: first, the land must not yet be inhabited by anyone; secondly, a man must occupy only the area required for his subsistence; thirdly, he must take possession of it, not by an empty ceremony, but by labour and cultivation, the only mark of ownership which, in default of legal title, ought to be respected by others.

Indeed, if we accord the right of first occupancy to necessity and labour, do we not extend it as far as it can go? Is it impossible to assign limits to this light? Will the mere setting foot on common ground be sufficient to give an immediate claim to the ownership of it? Will the power of driving away other men from it for a moment suffice to deprive them for ever of the right of returning to it? How can a man or a people take possession of an immense territory and rob the whole human race of it except by a punishable usurpation, since other men are deprived of the place of residence and the sustenance which nature gives to them in common? When Nuñez Balbao on the sea-shore took possession of the Pacific Ocean and of the whole of South America in the name of the crown of Castille, was this sufficient to dispossess all the inhabitants, and exclude from it all the princes in the world? On this supposition, such ceremonies might have been multiplied vainly enough; and the Catholic king in his cabinet might, by a single stroke, have taken possession of the whole world, only cutting off afterwards from his empire what was previously occupied by other princes.

We perceive how the lands of individuals, united and contiguous, become public territory, and how the right of sovereignty, extending itself from the subjects to the land which they occupy, becomes at once real and personal; which places the possessors in greater dependence, and makes their own powers a guarantee for their fidelity – an advantage which ancient monarchs do not appear to have clearly perceived, for, calling themselves only kings of the Persians or Scythians or Macedonians, they seem to have regarded themselves as chiefs of men rather than as owners of countries. Monarchs of today call themselves more cleverly kings of France, Spain, England, etc.; in thus holding the land they are quite sure of holding its inhabitants.

The peculiarity of this alienation is that the community, in receiving the property of individuals, so far from robbing them of it, only assures them lawful possession, and changes usurpation into true right, enjoyment into ownership. Also, the possessors being considered as depositaries of the public property, and their rights being respected by all the members of the state, as well as maintained by all its power against foreigners, they have, as it were, by a transfer advantageous to the public and still more to themselves, acquired all that they have given up – a paradox which is easily explained by distinguishing between the rights which the sovereign and the proprietor have over the same property, as we shall see hereafter.

It may also happen that men begin to unite before they possess anything, and that afterwards occupying territory sufficient for all, they enjoy it in common, or share it among themselves, either equally or in proportions fixed by the sovereign. In whatever way this acquisition is made, the right which every individual has over his own property is always subordinate to the right which the community has over all; otherwise there would be no stability in the social union, and no real force in the exercise of sovereignty.

I shall close this chapter and this book with a remark which ought to serve as a basis for the whole social system; it is that instead of destroying natural equality, the fundamental pact, on the contrary, substitutes a moral and lawful equality for the physical inequality which nature imposed upon men, so that, although unequal in strength or intellect, they all become equal by convention and legal right.*

* Under bad governments this equality is only apparent and illusory; it serves only to keep the poor in their misery and the rich in their usurpations. In fact, laws are always useful to those who possess and injurious to those that have nothing; whence it follows that the social state is advantageous to men only so far as they all have something, and none of them has too much.

24

BOOK TWO

CHAPTER 1

That Sovereignty is Inalienable

The first and most important consequence of the principles above established is that the general will alone can direct the forces of the state according to the object of its institution, which is the common good; for if the opposition of private interests has rendered necessary the establishment of societies, the agreement of these same interests has rendered it possible. That which is common to these different interests forms the social bond; and unless there were some point in which all interests agree, no society could exist. Now, it is solely with regard to this common interest that the society should be governed.

I say, then, that sovereignty, being nothing but the exercise of the general will, can never be alienated, and that the sovereign power, which is only a collective being, can be represented by itself alone; power indeed can be transmitted, but not will.

In fact, if it is not impossible that a particular will should agree on some point with the general will, it is at least impossible that this agreement should be lasting and constant; for the particular will naturally tends to preferences, and the general will to equality. It is still more impossible to have a security for this agreement; even though it should always exist, it would not be a result of art, but of chance. The sovereign may indeed say: 'I will now what a certain man wills, or at least what he says that he wills'; but he cannot say: 'What that man wills tomorrow, I shall also will', since it is absurd that the will should bind itself as regards the future, and since it is not incumbent on any will to consent to anything contrary to the welfare of the being that wills. If, then, the nation simply promises to obey, it dissolves itself by that act and loses its character as a people; the moment there is a master, there is no longer a sovereign, and forthwith the body politic is destroyed.

This does not imply that the orders of the chiefs cannot pass for decisions of the general will, so long as the sovereign, free to oppose them, refrains from doing so. In such a case the consent of the people should be inferred from the universal silence. This will be explained at greater length.

CHAPTER 2

That Sovereignty is Indivisible

For the same reason that sovereignty is inalienable it is indivisible; for the will is either general,* or it is not; it is either that of the body of the people, or that of only a portion. In the first case, this declared will is an act of sovereignty and constitutes law; in the second case, it is only a particular will, or an act of magistracy – it is at most a decree.

But our publicists, being unable to divide sovereignty in its principle, divide it in its object. They divide it into force and will, into legislative power and executive power; into rights of taxation, of justice, and of war; into internal administration and power of treating with foreigners – sometimes confounding all these departments, and sometimes separating them. They make the sovereign a fantastic being, formed of connected parts; it is as if they composed a man of several bodies, one with eyes, another with arms, another with feet, and nothing else. The Japanese conjurers, it is said, cut up a child before the eyes of the spectators; then, throwing all its limbs into the air, they make the child come down again alive and whole. Such almost are the jugglers' tricks of our publicists; after dismembering the social body, by a deception worthy of the fair, they recombine its parts, nobody knows how.

This error arises from their not having formed exact notions about the sovereign authority, and from their taking as parts of this authority what are only emanations from it. Thus, for example, the acts of declaring war and making peace have been regarded as acts of sovereignty, which is not the case, since neither of them is a law,

---

* That a will may be general, it is not always necessary that it should be unanimous, but it is necessary that all votes should be counted; any formal exclusion destroys the generality.

but only an application of the law, a particular act which determines the case of the law, as will be clearly seen when the idea attached to the word *law* is fixed.

By following out the other divisions in the same way, it would be found that, whenever the sovereignty appears divided, we are mistaken in our supposition; and that the rights which are taken as parts of that sovereignty are all subordinate to it, and always suppose supreme wills of which these rights are merely executive.

It would be impossible to describe the great obscurity in which this want of precision has involved the conclusions of writers on the subject of political right when they have endeavoured to decide upon the respective rights of kings and peoples on the principles that they had established. Everyone can see, in chapters III and IV of the first book of Grotius, how that learned man and his translator Barbeyrac become entangled and embarrassed in their sophisms, for fear of saying too much or not saying enough according to their views, and so offending the interests that they had to conciliate. Grotius, having taken refuge in France through discontent with his own country, and wishing to pay court to Louis XIII, to whom his book is dedicated, spares no pains to despoil the people of all their rights and, in the most artful manner, bestow them on kings. This also would clearly have been the inclination of Barbeyrac, who dedicated his translation to the king of England, George I. But unfortunately the expulsion of James II, which he calls an abdication, forced him to be reserved and to equivocate and evade, in order not to make William appear a usurper. If these two writers had adopted true principles, all difficulties would have been removed, and they would have been always consistent; but they would have spoken the truth with regret, and would have paid court only to the people. Truth, however, does not lead to fortune, and the people confer neither embassies, nor professorships, nor pensions.

CHAPTER 3

Whether the General Will Can Err

It follows from what precedes that the general will is always right and always tends to the public advantage; but it does not follow that the resolutions of the people have always the same rectitude. Men always desire their own good, but do not always discern it; the people are never corrupted, though often deceived, and it is only then that they seem to will what is evil.

There is often a great deal of difference between the will of all and the general will; the latter regards only the common interest, while the former has regard to private interests, and is merely a sum of particular wills; but take away from these same wills the pluses and minuses which cancel one another,* and the general will remains as the sum of the differences.

If the people came to a resolution when adequately informed and without any communication among the citizens, the general will would always result from the great number of slight differences, and the resolution would always be good. But when factions, partial associations, are formed to the detriment of the whole society, the will of each of these associations becomes general with reference to its members, and particular with reference to the state; it may then be said that there are no longer as many voters as there are men, but only as many voters as there are associations. The differences become less numerous and yield a less general result.

---

* 'Every interest,' says the Marquis d'Argenson, 'has different principles. The accord of two particular interests is formed by opposition to that of a third.' He might have added that the accord of all interests is formed by opposition to that of each. Unless there were different interests, the common interest would scarcely be felt and would never meet with any obstacle; everything would go of itself, and politics would cease to be an art.

Lastly, when one of these associations becomes so great that it predominates over all the rest, you no longer have as the result a sum of small differences, but a single difference; there is then no longer a general will, and the opinion which prevails is only a particular opinion.

It is important, then, in order to have a clear declaration of the general will, that there should be no partial association in the state, and that every citizen should express only his own opinion.* Such was the unique and sublime institution of the great Lycurgus. But if there are partial associations, it is necessary to multiply their number and prevent inequality, as Solon, Numa, and Servius did. These are the only proper precautions for ensuring that the general will may always be enlightened, and that the people may not be deceived.

---

* 'It is true,' says Machiavelli, 'that some divisions injure the state, while some are beneficial to it; those are injurious to it which are accompanied by cabals and factions; those assist it which are maintained without cabals, without factions. Since, therefore, no founder of a state can provide against enmities in it, he ought at least to provide that there shall be no cabals.' (*History of Florence*, Book VII)

CHAPTER 4

The Limits of the Sovereign Power

If the state or city is nothing but a moral person, the life of which consists in the union of its members, and if the most important of its cares is that of self-preservation, it needs a universal and compulsive force to move and dispose every part in the manner most expedient for the whole. As nature gives every man an absolute power over all his limbs, the social pact gives the body politic an absolute power over all its members; and it is this same power which, when directed by the general will, bears, as I said, the name of sovereignty.

But besides the public person, we have to consider the private persons who compose it, and whose life and liberty are naturally independent of it. The question, then, is to distinguish clearly between the respective rights of the citizens and of the sovereign,* as well as between the duties which the former have to fulfil in their capacity as subjects and the natural rights which they ought to enjoy in their character as men.

It is admitted that whatever part of his power, property, and liberty each one alienates by the social compact is only that part of the whole of which the use is important to the community, but we must also admit that the sovereign alone is judge of what is important.

All the services that a citizen can render to the state he owes to it as soon as the sovereign demands them; but the sovereign, on its part, cannot impose on its subjects any burden which is useless to the community; it cannot even wish to do so, for, by the law of

---

* Attentive readers, do not, I beg you, hastily charge me with contradiction here. I could not avoid it in terms owing to the poverty of the language, but wait.

reason, just as by the law of nature, nothing is done without a cause.

The engagements which bind us to the social body are obligatory only because they are mutual; and their nature is such that in fulfilling them we cannot work for others without also working for ourselves. Why is the general will always right, and why do all invariably desire the prosperity of each, unless it is because there is no one but appropriates to himself this word *each* and thinks of himself in voting on behalf of all? This proves that equality of rights and the notion of justice that it produces are derived from the preference which each gives to himself, and consequently from man's nature; that the general will, to be truly such, should be so in its object as well as in its essence; that it ought to proceed from all in order to be applicable to all; and that it loses its natural rectitude when it tends to some individual and determinate object, because in that case, judging of what is unknown to us, we have no true principle of equity to guide us.

Indeed, so soon as a particular fact or right is in question with regard to a point which has not been regulated by an anterior general convention, the matter becomes contentious; it is a process in which the private persons interested are one of the parties and the public the other, but in which I perceive neither the law which must be followed, nor the judge who should decide. It would be ridiculous in such a case to wish to refer the matter for an express decision of the general will, which can be nothing but the decision of one of the parties, and which, consequently, is for the other party only a will that is foreign, partial, and inclined on such an occasion to injustice as well as liable to error. Therefore, just as a particular will cannot represent the general will, the general will in turn changes its nature when it has a particular end, and cannot, as general, decide about either a person or a fact. When the people of Athens, for instance, elected or deposed their chiefs, decreed honours to one, imposed penalties on another, and by multitudes of particular decrees exercised indiscriminately all the functions of government, the people no longer had any general will properly so called; they no longer acted as a sovereign power, but as magistrates. This will appear contrary to common ideas, but I must be allowed time to expound my own.

From this we must understand that what generalises the will is not so much the number of voices as the common interest which unites them; for, under this system, each necessarily submits to the conditions which he imposes on others – an admirable union of interest and justice, which gives to the deliberations of the community a spirit of equity that seems to disappear in the discussion of any private affair, for want of a common interest to unite and identify the ruling principle of the judge with that of the party.

By whatever path we return to our principle we always arrive at the same conclusion, *viz.* that the social compact establishes among the citizens such an equality that they all pledge themselves under the same conditions and ought all to enjoy the same rights. Thus, by the nature of the compact, every act of sovereignty, that is, every authentic act of the general will, binds or favours equally all the citizens; so that the sovereign knows only the body of the nation, and distinguishes none of those that compose it.

What, then, is an act of sovereignty properly so called? It is not an agreement between a superior and an inferior, but an agreement of the body with each of its members; a lawful agreement, because it has the social contract as its foundation; equitable, because it is common to all; useful, because it can have no other object than the general welfare; and stable, because it has the public force and the supreme power as a guarantee. So long as the subjects submit only to such conventions, they obey no one, but simply their own will; and to ask how far the respective rights of the sovereign and citizens extend is to ask up to what point the latter can make engagements among themselves, each with all and all with each.

Thus we see that the sovereign power, wholly absolute, wholly sacred, and wholly inviolable as it is, does not, and cannot, pass the limits of general conventions, and that every man can fully dispose of what is left to him of his property and liberty by these conventions; so that the sovereign never has a right to burden one subject more than another, because then the matter becomes particular and his power is no longer competent.

These distinctions once admitted, so untrue is it that in the social contract there is on the part of individuals any real renunciation, that their situation, as a result of this contract, is in reality preferable to what it was before, and that, instead of an alienation, they have only made an advantageous exchange of an uncertain and precarious mode of existence for a better and more assured one, of natural independence for liberty, of the power to injure others for their own safety, and of their strength, which others might overcome, for a right which the social union renders inviolable. Their lives, also, which they have devoted to the state, are continually protected by it; and in exposing their lives for its defence, what do they do but restore what they have received from it? What do they do but what they would do more frequently and with more risk in the state of nature, when, engaging in inevitable struggles, they would defend at the peril of their lives their means of preservation? All have to fight for their country in case of need, it is true; but then no one ever has to fight for himself. Do we not gain, moreover, by incurring, for what ensures our safety, a part of the risks that we should have to incur for ourselves individually, as soon as we were deprived of it?

CHAPTER 5

The Right of Life and Death

It may be asked how individuals who have no right to dispose of their own lives can transmit to the sovereign that right which they do not possess. The question appears hard to solve only because it is badly stated. Every man has a right to risk his own life in order to preserve it. Has it ever been said that one who throws himself out of a window to escape from a fire is guilty of suicide? Has the crime, indeed, ever been imputed to a man who perishes in a storm, although, on embarking, he was not ignorant of the danger?

The social treaty has as its end the preservation of the contracting parties. He who desires the end desires also the means, and some risks, even some losses, are inseparable from these means. He who is willing to preserve his life at the expense of others ought also to give it up or them when necessary. Now, the citizen is not a judge of the peril to which the law requires that he should expose himself; and when the prince has said to him: 'It is expedient for the state that you should die', he ought to die, since it is only on this condition that he has lived in security up to that time, and since his life is no longer merely a gift of nature, but a conditional gift of the state.

The penalty of death inflicted on criminals may be regarded almost from the same point of view; it is in order not to be the victim of an assassin that a man consents to die if he becomes one. In this treaty, far from disposing of his own life, he thinks only of securing it, and it is not supposed that any of the contracting parties contemplates at the time being hanged.

Moreover, every evil-doer who attacks social rights becomes by his crimes a rebel and a traitor to his country; by violating its laws he ceases to be a member of it, and even makes war upon it. Then the preservation of the state is incompatible with his own – one of

THE SOCIAL CONTRACT [II,5]

the two must perish; and when a guilty man is executed, it is less as a citizen than as an enemy. The proceedings and the judgment are the proofs and the declaration that he has broken the social treaty, and consequently that he is no longer a member of the state. Now, as he has acknowledged himself to be such, at least by his residence, he ought to be cut off from it by exile as a violator of the compact, or by death as a public enemy; for such an enemy is not a moral person, he is simply a man; and this is a case in which the right of war is to slay the vanquished.

But, it will be said, the condemnation of a criminal is a particular act. Granted; but this condemnation does not belong to the sovereign; it is a right which that power can confer, though itself unable to exercise it. All my ideas are connected, but I could not expound them all at once.

Again, the frequency of capital punishments is always a sign of weakness or indolence in the government. There is no man so worthless that he cannot be made good for something. We have a right to kill, even for example's sake, only those who cannot be preserved without danger.

As regards the right to pardon or to exempt a guilty man from the penalty imposed by the law and inflicted by the judge, it belongs only to a power which is above both the judge and the law, that is to say, the sovereign; still its right in this is not very plain, and the occasions for exercising it are very rare. In a well-governed state there are few punishments, not because many pardons are granted, but because there are few criminals; the multitude of crimes ensures impunity when the state is decaying. Under the Roman Republic neither the Senate nor the consuls attempted to grant pardons; the people even did not grant any, although they sometimes revoked their own judgments. Frequent pardons proclaim that crimes will soon need them no longer, and everyone sees to what that leads. But I feel my heart murmuring and restraining my pen; let us leave these questions to be discussed by the just man who has not erred and who never needed pardon himself.

CHAPTER 6

The Law

By the social compact we have given existence and life to the body politic; the question now is to endow it with movement and will by legislation. For the original act by which this body is formed and consolidated determines nothing in addition as to what it must do for its own preservation.

What is right and conformable to order is such by the nature of things, and independently of human conventions. All justice comes from God, he alone is the source of it; but could we receive it direct from so lofty a source, we should need neither government nor laws. Without doubt there is a universal justice emanating from reason alone; but this justice, in order to be admitted among us, should be reciprocal. Regarding things from a human standpoint, the laws of justice are inoperative among men for want of a natural sanction; they only bring good to the wicked and evil to the just when the latter observe them with everyone, and no one observes them in return. Conventions and laws, then, are necessary to couple rights with duties and apply justice to its object. In the state of nature, where everything is in common, I owe nothing to those to whom I have promised nothing; I recognise as belonging to others only what is useless to me. This is not the case in the civil state, in which all rights are determined by law.

But then, finally, what is a law? So long as men are content to attach to this word only metaphysical ideas, they will continue to argue without being understood; and when they have stated what a law of nature is, they will know no better what a law of the state is.

I have already said that there is no general will with reference to a particular object. In fact, this particular object is either in the state or outside of it. If it is outside the state, a will which is foreign to it is not general in relation to it; and if it is within the state, it forms part of it; then there is formed between the whole and its part a relation which makes of it two separate beings, of which the part is one, and the whole, less this same part, is the other. But the whole less one part is not the whole, and so long as the relation subsists, there is no longer any whole, but two unequal parts; whence it follows that the will of the one is no longer general in relation to the other.

But when the whole people decree concerning the whole people, they consider themselves alone; and if a relation is then constituted, it is between the whole object under one point of view and the whole object under another point of view, without any division at all. Then the matter respecting which they decree is general like the will that decrees. It is this act that I call a law.

When I say that the object of the laws is always general, I mean that the law considers subjects collectively, and actions as abstract, never a man as an individual nor a particular action. Thus the law may indeed decree that there shall be privileges, but cannot confer them on any person by name; the law can create several classes of citizens, and even assign the qualifications which shall entitle them to rank in these classes, but it cannot nominate such and such persons to be admitted to them; it can establish a royal government and a hereditary succession, but cannot elect a king or appoint a royal family; in a word, no function which has reference to an individual object appertains to the legislative power.

From this standpoint we see immediately that it is no longer necessary to ask whose office it is to make laws, since they are acts of the general will; nor whether the prince is above the laws, since he is a member of the state; nor whether the law can be unjust, since no one is unjust to himself; nor how we are free and yet subject to the laws, since the laws are only registers of our wills.

We see, further, that since the law combines the universality of the will with the universality of the object, whatever any man prescribes on his own authority is not a law; and whatever the sovereign itself prescribes respecting a particular object is not a law, but a decree, not an act of sovereignty, but of magistracy.

I therefore call any state a republic which is governed by laws, under whatever form of administration it may be; for then only does the public interest predominate and the commonwealth

count for something. Every legitimate government is republican;*
I will explain hereafter what government is.

Laws are properly only the conditions of civil association. The
people, being subjected to the laws, should be the authors of them;
it concerns only the associates to determine the conditions of
association. But how will they be determined? Will it be by a
common agreement, by a sudden inspiration? Has the body politic
an organ for expressing its will? Who will give it the foresight
necessary to frame its acts and publish them at the outset? Or how
shall it declare them in the hour of need? How would a blind
multitude, which often knows not what it wishes because it rarely
knows what is good for it, execute of itself an enterprise so great, so
difficult, as a system of legislation? Of themselves, the people
always desire what is good, but do not always discern it. The
general will is always right, but the judgment which guides it is not
always enlightened. It must be made to see objects as they are,
sometimes as they ought to appear; it must be shown the good path
that it is seeking, and guarded from the seduction of private
interests; it must be made to observe closely times and places, and
to balance the attraction of immediate and palpable advantages
against the danger of remote and concealed evils. Individuals see
the good which they reject; the public desire the good which they
do not see. All alike have need of guides. The former must be
compelled to conform their wills to their reason; the people must
be taught to know what they require. Then from the public
enlightenment results the union of the understanding and the will
in the social body; and from that the close co-operation of the
parts, and, lastly, the maximum power of the whole. Hence arises
the need of a legislator.

---

* I do not mean by this word an aristocracy or democracy only, but in
general any government directed by the general will, which is the law. To be
legitimate, the government must not be combined with the sovereign power,
but must be its minister; then monarchy itself is a republic. This will be made
clear in the next book.

CHAPTER 7

The Legislator

In order to discover the rules of association that are most suitable to nations, a superior intelligence would be necessary who could see all the passions of men without experiencing any of them; who would have no affinity with our nature and yet know it thoroughly; whose happiness would not depend on us, and who would nevertheless be quite willing to interest himself in ours; and, lastly, one who, storing up for himself with the progress of time a far-off glory in the future, could labour in one age and enjoy in another.* Gods would be necessary to give laws to men.

The same argument that Caligula adduced as to fact, Plato put forward with regard to right, in order to give an idea of the civil or royal man whom he is in quest of in his work the *statesman*. But if it is true that a great prince is a rare man, what will a great legislator be? The first has only to follow the model which the other has to frame. The latter is the mechanician who invents the machine, the former is only the workman who puts it in readiness and works it. 'In the birth of societies,' says Montesquieu, 'it is the chiefs of the republics who frame the institutions, and afterwards it is the institutions which mould the chiefs of the republics.'

He who dares undertake to give institutions to a nation ought to feel himself capable, as it were, of changing human nature; of transforming every individual, who in himself is a complete and independent whole, into part of a greater whole from which he receives in some manner his life and his being; of altering man's

* A nation becomes famous only when its legislation is beginning to decline. We are ignorant during how many centuries the institutions of Lycurgus conferred happiness on the Spartans before they were known in the rest of Greece.

constitution in order to strengthen it; of substituting a social and moral existence for the independent and physical existence which we have all received from nature. In a word, it is necessary to deprive man of his native powers in order to endow him with some which are alien to him, and of which he cannot make use without the aid of other people. The more thoroughly those natural powers are deadened and destroyed, the greater and more durable are the acquired powers, the more solid and perfect also are the institutions; so that if every citizen is nothing, and can be nothing, except in combination with all the rest, and if the force acquired by the whole be equal or superior to the sum of the natural forces of all the individuals, we may say that legislation is at the highest point of perfection which it can attain.

The legislator is in all respects an extraordinary man in the state. If he ought to be so by his genius, he is not less so by his office. It is not magistracy nor sovereignty. This office, which constitutes the republic, does not enter into its constitution; it is a special and superior office, having nothing in common with human government; for, if he who rules men ought not to control legislation, he who controls legislation ought not to rule men; otherwise his laws, being ministers of his passions, would often serve only to perpetuate his acts of injustice; he would never be able to prevent private interests from corrupting the sacredness of his work.

When Lycurgus gave laws to his country, he began by abdicating his royalty. It was the practice of the majority of the Greek towns to entrust to foreigners the framing of their laws. The modern republics of Italy often imitated this usage; that of Geneva did the same and found it advantageous.* Rome, at her most glorious epoch, saw all the crimes of tyranny spring up in her bosom, and saw herself on the verge of destruction, through uniting in the same hands legislative authority and sovereign power.

---

* Those who consider Calvin only as a theologian are but little acquainted with the extent of his genius. The preparation of our wise edicts, in which he had a large share, does him as much credit as his *Institutes*. Whatever revolution time may bring about in our religion, so long as love of country and of liberty is not extinct among us, the memory of that great man will not cease to be revered.

Yet the Decemvirs themselves never arrogated the right to pass any law on their sole authority. Nothing that we propose to you, they said to the people, can pass into law without your consent. Romans, be yourselves the authors of the laws which are to secure your happiness.

He who frames laws, then, has, or ought to have, no legislative right, and the people themselves cannot, even if they wished, divest themselves of this incommunicable right, because, according to the fundamental compact, it is only the general will that binds individuals, and we can never be sure that a particular will is conformable to the general will until it has been submitted to the free votes of the people. I have said this already, but it is not useless to repeat it.

Thus we find simultaneously in the work of legislation two things that seem incompatible – an enterprise surpassing human powers, and, to execute it, an authority that is a mere nothing.

Another difficulty deserves attention. Wise men who want to speak to the vulgar in their own language instead of in a popular way will not be understood. Now, there are a thousand kinds of ideas which it is impossible to translate into the language of the people. Views very general and objects very remote are alike beyond its reach; and each individual, approving of no other plan of government than that which promotes his own interests, does not readily perceive the benefits that he is to derive from the continual deprivations which good laws impose. In order that a newly formed nation might approve sound maxims of politics and observe the fundamental rules of state policy, it would be necessary that the effect should become the cause; that the social spirit, which should be the work of the institution, should preside over the institution itself, and that men should be, prior to the laws, what they ought to become by means of them. Since, then, the legislator cannot employ either force or reasoning, he must needs have recourse to an authority of a different order, which can compel without violence and persuade without convincing.

It is this which in all ages has constrained the founders of nations to resort to the intervention of heaven, and to give the gods the credit for their own wisdom, in order that the nations subjected to the laws of the state as to those of nature, and recognising the same power in the formation of man and in that of the state, might obey willingly, and bear submissively the yoke of the public welfare.

The legislator puts into the mouths of the immortals that sublime reason which soars beyond the reach of common men, in order that he may win over by divine authority those whom human prudence could not move.* But it does not belong to every man to make the gods his oracles, nor to be believed when he proclaims himself their interpreter. The great soul of the legislator is the real miracle which must give proof of his mission. Any man can engrave tables of stone, or bribe an oracle, or pretend secret intercourse with some divinity, or train a bird to speak in his ear, or find some other clumsy means to impose on the people. He who is acquainted with such means only will perchance be able to assemble a crowd of foolish persons; but he will never found an empire, and his extravagant work will speedily perish with him. Empty deceptions form but a transient bond; it is only wisdom that makes it lasting. The Jewish law, which still endures, and that of the child of Ishmael, which for ten centuries has ruled half the world, still bear witness today to the great men who dictated them; and whilst proud philosophy or blind party spirit sees in them nothing but fortunate impostors, the true statesman admires in their systems the great and powerful genius which directs durable institutions.

It is not necessary from all this to infer with Warburton that politics and religion have among us a common aim, but only that, in the origin of nations, one serves as an instrument of the other.

---

* 'It is true,' says Machiavelli, 'there never was in a nation any promulgator of extraordinary laws who had not recourse to God, because otherwise they would not have been accepted; for there are many advantages recognised by a wise man which are not so self-evident that they can convince others.' (*Discourses on Titus Livius*, Book I, chapter 11)

CHAPTER 8

The People

As an architect, before erecting a large edifice, examines and tests the soil in order to see whether it can support the weight, so a wise lawgiver does not begin by drawing up laws that are good in themselves, but considers first whether the people for whom he designs them are fit to endure them. It is on this account that Plato refused to legislate for the Arcadians and Cyrenians, knowing that these two peoples were rich and could not tolerate equality; and it is on this account that good laws and worthless men were to be found in Crete, for Minos had only disciplined a people steeped in vice.

A thousand nations that have flourished on the earth could never have borne good laws; and even those that might have done so could have succeeded for only a very short period of their whole duration. The majority of nations, as well as of men, are tractable only in their youth; they become incorrigible as they grow old. When once customs are established and prejudices have taken root, it is a perilous and futile enterprise to try and reform them; for the people cannot even endure that their evils should be touched with a view to their removal, like those stupid and cowardly patients that shudder at the sight of a physician.

But just as some diseases unhinge men's minds and deprive them of all remembrance of the past, so we sometimes find, during the existence of states, epochs of violence, in which revolutions produce an influence upon nations such as certain crises produce upon individuals, in which horror of the past supplies the place of forgetfulness, and in which the state, inflamed by civil wars, springs forth so to speak from its ashes, and regains the vigour of youth in issuing from the arms of death. Such was Sparta in the time of Lycurgus, such was Rome after the Tarquins, and such among us moderns were Holland and Switzerland after the expulsion of their tyrants.

But these events are rare; they are exceptions, the explanation of which is always found in the particular constitution of the excepted state. They could not even happen twice with the same nation; for it may render itself free so long as it is merely barbarous, but can no longer do so when the resources of the state are exhausted. Then commotions may destroy it without revolutions being able to restore it, and as soon as its chains are broken, it falls in pieces and ceases to exist; henceforward it requires a master and not a deliverer. Free nations, remember this maxim: 'Liberty may be acquired but never recovered.'

Youth is not infancy. There is for nations as for men a period of youth, or, if you will, of maturity, which they must await before they are subjected to laws; but it is not always easy to discern when a people is mature, and if the time is anticipated, the labour is abortive. One nation is governable from its origin, another is not so at the end of ten centuries. The Russians will never be really civilised, because they have been civilised too early. Peter had an imitative genius; he had not the true genius that creates and produces anything from nothing. Some of his measures were beneficial, but the majority were ill-timed. He saw that his people were barbarous, but he did not see that they were unripe for civilisation; he wished to civilise them, when it was necessary only to discipline them. He wished to produce at once Germans or Englishmen, when he should have begun by making Russians; he prevented his subjects from ever becoming what they might have been, by persuading them that they were what they were not. It is in this way that a French tutor trains his pupil to shine for a moment in childhood, and then to be for ever a nonentity. The Russian Empire will desire to subjugate Europe, and will itself be subjugated. The Tartars, its subjects or neighbours, will become its masters and ours. This revolution appears to me inevitable. All the kings of Europe are working in concert to accelerate it.

CHAPTER 9

The People (continued)

As nature has set limits to the stature of a properly formed man, outside which it produces only giants and dwarfs; so likewise, with regard to the best constitution of a state, there are limits to its possible extent so that it may be neither too great to enable it to be well governed, nor too small to enable it to maintain itself single-handed. There is in every body politic a maximum of force which it cannot exceed, and which is often diminished as the state is aggrandised. The more the social bond is extended, the more it is weakened; and, in general, a small state is proportionally stronger than a large one.

A thousand reasons demonstrate the truth of this maxim. In the first place, administration becomes more difficult at great distances, as a weight becomes heavier at the end of a longer lever. It also becomes more burdensome in proportion as its parts are multi-plied; for every town has first its own administration, for which the people pay; every district has its administration, still paid for by the people; next, every province, then the superior governments, the satrapies, the vice-royalties, which must be paid for more dearly as we ascend, and always at the cost of the unfortunate people; lastly comes the supreme administration, which overwhelms everything. So many additional burdens perpetually exhaust the subjects; and far from being better governed by all these different orders, they are much worse governed than if they had but a single superior. Meanwhile, hardly any resources remain for cases of emergency; and when it is necessary to have recourse to them the state trembles on the brink of ruin.

Nor is this all; not only has the government less vigour and activity in enforcing observance of the laws, in putting a stop to vexations, in reforming abuses, and in forestalling seditious enterprises which may

be entered upon in distant places; but the people have less affection
for their chiefs whom they never see, for their country, which is in
their eyes like the world, and for their fellow-citizens, most of
whom are strangers to them. The same laws cannot be suitable to so
many different provinces, which have different customs and different climates, and cannot tolerate the same form of government.
Different laws beget only trouble and confusion among the nations
which, living under the same chiefs and in constant communication,
mingle or intermarry with one another, and, when subjected to
other usages, never know whether their patrimony is really theirs.
Talents are hidden, virtues ignored, vices unpunished, in that multitude of men, unknown to one another, whom the seat of the
supreme administration gathers together in one place. The chiefs,
overwhelmed with business, see nothing themselves; clerks rule the
state. In a word, the measures that must be taken to maintain the
general authority, which so many officers at a distance wish to evade
or impose upon, absorb all the public attention; no regard for the
welfare of the people remains, and scarcely any for their defence in
time of need; and thus a body too huge for its constitution sinks and
perishes, crushed by its own weight.

On the other hand, the state must secure a certain foundation,
that it may possess stability and resist the shocks which it will
infallibly experience, as well as sustain the efforts which it will be
forced to make in order to maintain itself; for all nations have a
kind of centrifugal force, by which they continually act one against
another, and tend to aggrandise themselves at the expense of their
neighbours, like the vortices of Descartes. Thus the weak are in
danger of being quickly swallowed up, and none can preserve itself
long except by putting itself in a kind of equilibrium with all,
which renders the compression almost equal everywhere.

Hence we see that there are reasons for expansion and reasons for
contraction; and it is not the least of a statesman's talents to find the
proportion between the two which is most advantageous for the
preservation of the state. We may say, in general, that the former,
being only external and relative, ought to be subordinated to the
others, which are internal and absolute. A healthy and strong
constitution is the first thing to be sought; and we should rely more
on the vigour that springs from a good government than on the
resources furnished by an extensive territory.

States have, however, been constituted in such a way that the necessity of making conquests entered into their very constitution, and in order to maintain themselves they were forced to enlarge themselves continually. Perhaps they rejoiced greatly at this happy necessity, which nevertheless revealed to them, with the limit of their greatness, the inevitable moment of their fall.

CHAPTER 10

The People (continued)

A body politic may be measured in two ways, *viz.* by the extent of its territory, and by the number of its people; and there is between these two modes of measurement a suitable relation according to which the state may be assigned its true dimensions. It is the men that constitute the state, and it is the soil that sustains the men; the due relation, then, is that the land should suffice for the maintenance of its inhabitants, and that there should be as many inhabitants as the land can sustain. In this proportion is found the maximum power of a given number of people; for if there is too much land, the care of it is burdensome, the cultivation inadequate, and the produce superfluous, and this is the proximate cause of defensive wars. If there is not enough land, the state is at the mercy of its neighbours for the additional quantity; and this is the proximate cause of offensive wars. Any nation which has, by its position, only the alternative between commerce and war is weak in itself; it is dependent on its neighbours and on events; it has only a short and precarious existence. It conquers and changes its situation, or it is conquered and reduced to nothing. It can preserve its freedom only by virtue of being small or great.

It is impossible to express numerically a fixed ratio between the extent of land and the number of men which are reciprocally sufficient, on account of the differences that are found in the quality of the soil, in its degrees of fertility, in the nature of its products, and in the influence of climate, as well as on account of those which we observe in the constitutions of the inhabitants, of whom some consume little in a fertile country, while others consume much on an unfruitful soil. Further, attention must be paid to the greater or less fecundity of the women, to the conditions of the country, whether more or less favourable to population, and to the numbers which the legislator may hope to draw thither by his institutions; so that an opinion should be based not on what is seen, but on what is foreseen, while the actual state of the people should be less observed than that which it ought naturally to attain. In short, there are a thousand occasions on which the particular accidents of situation require or permit that more territory than appears necessary should be taken up. Thus men will spread out a good deal in a mountainous country, where the natural productions, *viz*. woods and pastures, require less labour, where experience teaches that women are more fecund than in the plains, and where with an extensive inclined surface there is only a small horizontal base, which alone should count for vegetation. On the other hand, people may inhabit a smaller space on the sea-shore, even among rocks and sands that are almost barren, because fishing can, in great measure, supply the deficiency in the productions of the earth, because men ought to be more concentrated in order to repel pirates, and because, further, it is easier to relieve the country, by means of colonies, of the inhabitants with which it is overburdened.

In order to establish a nation, it is necessary to add to these conditions one which cannot supply the place of any other, but without which they are all useless – it is that the people should enjoy abundance and peace; for the time of a state's formation is, like that of forming soldiers in a square, the time when the body is least capable of resistance and most easy to destroy. Resistance would be greater in a state of absolute disorder than at a moment of fermentation, when each is occupied with his own position and not with the common danger. Should a war, a famine, or a sedition supervene at this critical period, the state is inevitably overthrown.

Many governments, indeed, may be established during such storms, but then it is these very governments that destroy the state. Usurpers always bring about or select troublous times for passing, under cover of the public agitation, destructive laws which the people would never adopt when sober-minded. The choice of the moment for the establishment of a government is one of the surest marks for distinguishing the work of the legislator from that of the tyrant.

What nation, then, is adapted for legislation? That which is already united, by some bond of interest, origin, or convention, but has not yet borne the real yoke of the laws; that which has no fear of being overwhelmed by a sudden invasion, but which, without entering into the disputes of its neighbours, can single-handed resist either of them, or aid one in repelling the other; that in which every member can be known by all, and in which there is no necessity to lay on a man a greater burden than a man can bear; that which can subsist without other nations, and without which every other nation can subsist;* that which is neither rich nor poor and is self-sufficing; lastly, that which combines the stability of an old nation with the docility of a new one. The work of legislation is rendered arduous not so much by what must be established as by what must be destroyed; and that which makes success so rare is the impossibility of finding the simplicity of nature conjoined with the necessities of society. All these conditions, it is true, are with difficulty combined; hence few well-constituted states are seen.

There is still one country in Europe capable of legislation; it is the island of Corsica. The courage and firmness which that brave nation has exhibited in recovering and defending its freedom would well deserve that some wise man should teach it how to preserve it. I have some presentiment that this small island will one day astonish Europe.

---

* If of two neighbouring nations one could not subsist without the other, it would be a very hard situation for the first, and a very dangerous one for the second. Every wise nation in such a case will endeavour very quickly to free the other from this dependence. The republic of Thlascala, enclosed in the empire of Mexico, preferred to do without salt rather than buy it of the Mexicans or even accept it gratuitously. The wise Thlascalans saw a trap hidden beneath this generosity. They kept themselves free; and this small state, enclosed in that great empire, was at last the instrument of its downfall.

CHAPTER 11

The Different Systems of Legislation

If we ask precisely wherein consists the greatest good of all, which ought to be the aim of every system of legislation, we shall find that it is summed up in two principal objects, *liberty* and *equality* – liberty, because any individual dependence is so much force withdrawn from the body of the state; equality, because liberty cannot subsist without it.

I have already said what civil liberty is. With regard to equality, we must not understand by this word that the degrees of power and wealth should be absolutely the same; but that, as to power, it should fall short of all violence, and never be exercised except by virtue of station and of the laws; while, as to wealth, no citizen should be rich enough to be able to buy another, and none poor enough to be forced to sell himself,* which supposes, on the part of the great, moderation in property and influence, and, on the part of ordinary citizens, repression of avarice and covetousness.

It is said that this equality is a chimera of speculation which cannot exist in practical affairs. But if the abuse is inevitable, does it follow that it is unnecessary even to regulate it? It is precisely because the force of circumstances is ever tending to destroy equality that the force of legislation should always tend to maintain it.

But these general objects of every good institution ought to be modified in each country by the relations which arise both from the local situation and from the character of the inhabitants; and it is with reference to these relations that we must assign to each nation a

---

* If, then, you wish to give stability to the state, bring the two extremes as near together as possible; tolerate neither rich people nor beggars. These two conditions, naturally inseparable, are equally fatal to the general welfare; from the one class spring tyrants, from the other, the supporters of tyranny; it is always between these that the traffic in public liberty is carried on; the one buys and the other sells.

particular system of institutions, which shall be the best, not perhaps in itself, but for the state for which it is designed. For instance, if the soil is unfruitful and barren, or the country too confined for its inhabitants, turn your attention to arts and manufactures, and exchange their products for the provisions that you require. On the other hand, if you occupy rich plains and fertile slopes, if, in a productive region, you are in need of inhabitants, bestow all your cares on agriculture, which multiplies men, and drive out the arts, which would only end in depopulating the country by gathering together in a few spots the few inhabitants that the land possesses.* If you occupy extensive and convenient coasts, cover the sea with vessels and foster commerce and navigation; you will have a short and brilliant existence. If the sea on your coasts bathes only rocks that are almost inaccessible, remain fish-eating barbarians; you will lead more peaceful, perhaps better, and certainly happier lives. In a word, besides the maxims common to all, each nation contains within itself some cause which influences it in a particular way, and renders its legislation suitable for it alone. Thus the Hebrews in ancient times, and the Arabs more recently, had religion as their chief object, the Athenians literature, Carthage and Tyre commerce, Rhodes navigation, Sparta war, Rome valour. The author of the *Spirit of the Laws* has shown in a multitude of instances by what arts the legislator directs his institutions towards each of these objects.

What renders the constitution of a state really solid and durable is the observance of expediency in such a way that natural relations and the laws always coincide, the latter only serving, as it were, to secure, support, and rectify the former. But if the legislator, mistaken in his object, takes a principle different from that which springs from the nature of things; if the one tends to servitude, the other to liberty, the one to riches, the other to population, the one to peace, the other to conquests, we shall see the laws imperceptibly weakened and the constitution impaired; and the state will be ceaselessly agitated until it is destroyed or changed, and invincible nature has resumed her sway.

---

* Any branch of foreign commerce, says the Marquis d'Argenson, diffuses merely a deceptive utility through the kingdom generally; it may enrich a few individuals, even a few towns, but the nation as a whole gains nothing, and the people are none the better for it.

CHAPTER 12

Division of the Laws

In order that everything may be duly regulated and the best possible form given to the commonwealth, there are various relations to be considered. First, the action of the whole body acting on itself, that is, the relation of the whole to the whole, or of the sovereign to the state; and this relation is composed of that of the intermediate terms, as we shall see hereafter.

The laws governing this relation bear the name of political laws, and are also called fundamental laws, not without some reason if they are wise ones; for, if in every state there is only one good method of regulating it, the people which has discovered it ought to adhere to it; but if the established order is bad, why should we regard as fundamental laws which prevent it from being good? Besides, in any case, a nation is always at liberty to change its laws, even the best; for if it likes to injure itself, who has a right to prevent it from doing so?

The second relation is that of the members with one another, or with the body as a whole; and this relation should, in respect of the first, be as small, and, in respect of the second, as great as possible; so that every citizen may be perfectly independent of all the rest, and in absolute dependence on the state. And this is always effected by the same means; for it is only the power of the state that secures the freedom of its members. It is from this second relation that civil laws arise.

We may consider a third kind of relation between the individual man and the law, *viz*. that of punishable disobedience; and this gives rise to the establishment of criminal laws, which at bottom are not so much a particular species of laws as the sanction of all the others.

To these three kinds of laws is added a fourth, the most important of all, which is graven neither on marble nor on brass, but in the hearts of the citizens; a law which creates the real constitution of the state, which acquires new strength daily, which, when other laws grow obsolete or pass away, revives them or supplies their place, preserves a people in the spirit of their institutions, and imperceptibly substitutes the force of habit for that of authority. I speak of manners, customs, and above all of opinion – a province unknown to our politicians, but one on which the success of all the rest depends; a province with which the great legislator is occupied in private, while he appears to confine himself to particular regulations, that are merely the arching of the vault, of which manners, slow to develop, form at length the immovable keystone.

Of these different classes, political laws, which constitute the form of government, alone relate to my subject.

BOOK THREE

Before speaking of the different forms of government, let us try to fix the precise meaning of that word, which has not yet been very clearly explained.

CHAPTER 1

Government in General

I warn the reader that this chapter must be read carefully, and that I do not know the art of making myself intelligible to those that will not be attentive.

Every free action has two causes concurring to produce it; the one moral, *viz.* the will which determines the act; the other physical, *viz.* the power which executes it. When I walk towards an object, I must first will to go to it; in the second place, my feet must carry me to it. Should a paralytic wish to run, or an active man not wish to do so, both will remain where they are. The body politic has the same motive powers; in it, likewise, force and will are distinguished, the latter under the name of *legislative power*, the former under the name of *executive power*. Nothing is, or ought to be, done in it without their co-operation.

We have seen that the legislative power belongs to the people and can belong to it alone. On the other hand, it is easy to see from the principles already established, that the executive power cannot belong to the people generally as legislative or sovereign, because that power is exerted only in particular acts, which are not within the province of the law, nor consequently within that of the sovereign, all the acts of which must be laws.

The public force, then, requires a suitable agent to concentrate it and put it in action according to the directions of the general will, to serve as a means of communication between the state and the sovereign, to effect in some manner in the public person what the union of soul and body effects in a man. This is, in the state, the function of the government, improperly confounded with the sovereign of which it is only the minister.

What, then, is the government? An intermediate body established between the subjects and the sovereign for their mutual correspondence, charged with the execution of the laws and with the maintenance of liberty both civil and political.

The members of this body are called magistrates or *kings*, that is, *governors*; and the body as a whole bears the name of *Prince*.* Those therefore who maintain that the act by which a people submits to its chiefs is not a contract are quite right. It is absolutely nothing but a commission, an employment, in which, as simple officers of the sovereign, they exercise in its name the power of which it has made them depositaries, and which it can limit, modify, and resume when it pleases. The alienation of such a right, being incompatible with the nature of the social body, is contrary to the object of the association.

Consequently, I give the name *government* or supreme administration to the legitimate exercise of the executive power, and that of Prince or magistrate to the man or body charged with that administration.

It is in the government that are found the intermediate powers, the relations of which constitute the relation of the whole to the whole, or of the sovereign to the state. This last relation can be represented by that of the extremes of a continued proportion, of which the mean proportional is the government. The government receives from the sovereign the commands which it gives to the people; and in order that the state may be in stable equilibrium, it is necessary, everything being balanced, that there should be equality between the product or the power of the government taken by itself, and the product or the power of the citizens, who are sovereign in the one aspect and subjects in the other.

Further, we could not alter any of the three terms without at once destroying the proportion. If the sovereign wishes to govern, or if the magistrate wishes to legislate, or if the subjects refuse to obey, disorder succeeds order, force and will no longer act in concert, and the state being dissolved falls into despotism or

---

* It is for this reason that at Venice the title of Most Serene Prince is given to the College, even when the Doge does not attend it.

anarchy. Lastly, as there is but one mean proportional between each relation, there is only one good government possible in a state; but as a thousand events may change the relations of a people, not only may different governments be good for different peoples, but for the same people at different times.

To try and give an idea of the different relations that may exist between these two extremes, I will take for an example the number of the people, as a relation most easy to express.

Let us suppose that the state is composed of ten thousand citizens. The sovereign can only be considered collectively and as a body; but every private person, in his capacity of subject, is considered as an individual; therefore the sovereign is to the subject as ten thousand is to one, that is, each member of the state has as his share only one ten-thousandth part of the sovereign authority, although he is entirely subjected to it.

If the nation consists of a hundred thousand men, the position of the subjects does not change, and each alike is subjected to the whole authority of the laws, whilst his vote, reduced to one hundred-thousandth, has ten times less influence in their enactment. The subject, then, always remaining a unit, the proportional power of the sovereign increases in the ratio of the number of the citizens. Whence it follows that the more the state is enlarged, the more does liberty diminish.

When I say that the proportional power increases, I mean that it is farther removed from equality. Therefore, the greater the ratio is in the geometrical sense, the less is the ratio in the common acceptation; in the former, the ratio, considered according to quantity, is measured by the exponent, and in the other, considered according to identity, it is estimated by the similarity.

Now, the less the particular wills correspond with the general will, that is, customs with laws, the more should the repressive power be increased. The government, then, in order to be effective, should be relatively stronger in proportion as the people are more numerous.

On the other hand, as the aggrandisement of the state gives the depositaries of the public authority more temptations and more opportunities to abuse their power, the more force should the government have to restrain the people, and the more should the sovereign have in its turn to restrain the government. I do not speak here of absolute force, but of the relative force of the different parts of the state.

It follows from this double ratio that the continued proportion between the sovereign, the Prince, and the people is not an arbitrary idea, but a necessary consequence of the nature of the body politic. It follows, further, that one of the extremes, *viz.* the people, as subject, being fixed and represented by unity, whenever the double ratio increases or diminishes, the single ratio increases or diminishes in like manner, and consequently the middle term is changed. This shows that there is no unique and absolute constitution of government, but that there may be as many governments different in nature as there are states different in size.

If, for the sake of turning this system to ridicule, it should be said that, in order to find this mean proportional and form the body of the government, it is, according to me, only necessary to take the square root of the number of the people, I should answer that I take that number here only as an example; that the ratios of which I speak are not measured only by the number of men, but in general by the quantity of action, which results from the combination of multitudes of causes; that, moreover, if for the purpose of expressing myself in fewer words, I borrow for a moment geometrical terms, I am nevertheless aware that geometrical precision has no place in moral quantities.

The government is on a small scale what the body politic which includes it is on a large scale. It is a moral person endowed with certain faculties, active like the sovereign, passive like the state, and it can be resolved into other similar relations; from which arises as a consequence a new proportion, and yet another within this, according to the order of the magistracies, until we come to an indivisible middle term, that is, to a single chief or supreme magistrate, who may be represented, in the middle of this progression, as unity between the series of fractions and that of the whole numbers.

Without embarrassing ourselves with this multiplication of terms, let us be content to consider the government as a new body in the state, distinct from the people and from the sovereign, and intermediate between the two.

There is this essential difference between those two bodies, that the state exists by itself, while the government exists only through the sovereign. Thus the dominant will of the Prince is, or ought to be, only the general will, or the law; its force is only the public force concentrated in itself; so soon as it wishes to perform of itself some absolute and independent act, the connection of the whole begins to be relaxed. If, lastly, the Prince should chance to have a particular will more active than that of the sovereign, and if, to enforce obedience to this particular will, it should employ the public force which is in its hands, in such a manner that there would be so to speak two sovereigns, the one *de jure* and the other *de facto*, the social union would immediately disappear, and the body politic would be dissolved.

Further, in order that the body of the government may have an existence, a real life, to distinguish it from the body of the state; in order that all its members may be able to act in concert and fulfil the object for which it is instituted, a particular personality is necessary to it, a feeling common to its members, a force, a will of its own tending to its preservation. This individual existence supposes assemblies, councils, a power of deliberating and resolving, rights, titles, and privileges which belong to the Prince exclusively, and which render the position of the magistrate more honourable in proportion as it is more arduous. The difficulty lies in the method of disposing, within the whole, this subordinate whole, in such a way that it may not weaken the general constitution in strengthening its own; that its particular force, intended for its own preservation, may always be kept distinct from the public force, designed for the preservation of the state; and, in a word, that it may always be ready to sacrifice the government to the people, and not the people to the government.

Moreover, although the artificial body of the government is the work of another artificial body, and has in some respects only a derivative and subordinate existence, that does not prevent it from acting with more or less vigour or celerity, from enjoying, so to speak, more or less robust health. Lastly, without directly departing from the object for which it was instituted, it may deviate from it more or less, according to the manner in which it is constituted.

From all these differences arise the different relations which the government must have with the body of the state, so as to accord with the accidental and particular relations by which the state itself is modified. For often the government that is best in itself will become the most vicious, unless its relations are changed so as to meet the defects of the body politic to which it belongs.

CHAPTER 2

The Principle which Constitutes the Different Forms of Government

To explain the general cause of these differences, I must here distinguish the Prince from the government, as I before distinguished the state from the sovereign.

The body of the magistracy may be composed of a greater or less number of members. We said that the ratio of the sovereign to the subjects was so much greater as the people were more numerous; and, by an evident analogy, we can say the same of the government with regard to the magistrates.

Now, the total force of the government, being always that of the state, does not vary: whence it follows that the more it employs this force on its own members, the less remains for operating upon the whole people.

Consequently, the more numerous the magistrates are, the weaker is the government. As this maxim is fundamental, let us endeavour to explain it more clearly.

We can distinguish in the person of the magistrate three wills essentially different: first, the will peculiar to the individual, which tends only to his personal advantage; secondly, the common will of the magistrates, which has reference solely to the advantage of the Prince, and which may be called the corporate will, being general in relation to the government, and particular in relation to the state of which the government forms part; in the third place, the will of the people, or the sovereign will, which is general both in relation to the state considered as the whole, and in relation to the government considered as part of the whole.

In a perfect system of legislation the particular or individual will should be inoperative; the corporate will proper to the government quite subordinate; and consequently the general or sovereign will always dominant, and the sole rule of all the rest.

On the other hand, according to the natural order, these different wills become more active in proportion as they are concentrated. Thus the general will is always the weakest, the corporate will has the second rank, and the particular will the first of all; so that in the government each member is, firstly, himself, next a magistrate, and then a citizen – a gradation directly opposed to that which the social order requires.

But suppose that the whole government is in the hands of a single man, then the particular will and the corporate will are perfectly united, and consequently the latter is in the highest possible degree of intensity. Now, as it is on the degree of will that the exertion of force depends, and as the absolute power of the government does not vary, it follows that the most active government is that of a single person.

On the other hand, let us unite the government with the legislative authority; let us make the sovereign the Prince, and all the citizens magistrates; then the corporate will, confounded with the general will, will have no more activity than the latter, and will leave the particular will in all its force. Thus the government, always with the same absolute force, will be at its minimum of relative force or activity.

These relations are incontestable, and other considerations serve still further to confirm them. We see, for example, that each magistrate is more active in his body than each citizen is in his, and that consequently the particular will has much more influence in the acts of government than in those of the sovereign; for every magistrate is almost always charged with some function of government, whereas each citizen, taken by himself, has no function of sovereignty. Besides, the more a state extends, the more is its real force increased, although it does not increase in proportion to its extent; but, while the state remains the same, it is useless to multiply magistrates, for the government acquires no greater real force, inasmuch as this force is that of the state, the quantity of which is always uniform. Thus the relative force or activity of the government diminishes without its absolute or real force being able to increase.

It is certain, moreover, that the despatch of business is retarded in proportion as more people are charged with it; that, in laying too much stress on prudence, we leave too little to fortune; that opportunities are allowed to pass by, and that owing to excessive deliberation the fruits of deliberation are often lost.

I have just shown that the government is weakened in proportion to the multiplication of magistrates, and I have before demonstrated that the more numerous the people is, the more ought the repressive force to be increased. Whence it follows that the ratio between the magistrates and the government ought to be inversely as the ratio between the subjects and the sovereign; that is, the more the state is enlarged, the more should the government contract; so that the number of chiefs should diminish in proportion as the number of the people is increased.

But I speak here only of the relative force of the government, and not of its rectitude; for, on the other hand, the more numerous the magistracy is, the more does the corporate will approach the general will; whereas, under a single magistrate, this same corporate will is, as I have said, only a particular will. Thus, what is lost on one side can be gained on the other, and the art of the legislator consists in knowing how to fix the point where the force and will of the government, always in reciprocal proportion, are combined in the ratio most advantageous to the state.

CHAPTER 3

Classification of Governments

We have seen in the previous chapter why the different kinds or forms of government are distinguished by the number of members that compose them; it remains to be seen in the present chapter how this division is made.

The sovereign may, in the first place, commit the charge of the government to the whole people, or to the greater part of the people, in such a way that there may be more citizens who are magistrates than simple individual citizens. We call this form of government a *democracy*.

Or it may confine the government to a small number, so that there may be more ordinary citizens than magistrates; and this form bears the name of *aristocracy*.

Lastly, it may concentrate the whole government in the hands of a single magistrate from whom all the rest derive their power. This third form is the most common, and is called *monarchy*, or royal government.

We should remark that all these forms, or at least the first two, admit of degrees, and may indeed have a considerable range; for democracy may embrace the whole people, or be limited to a half. Aristocracy, in its turn, may restrict itself from a half of the people to the smallest number indeterminately. Royalty even is susceptible of some division. Sparta by its constitution always had two kings; and in the Roman Empire there were as many as eight Emperors at once without its being possible to say that the Empire was divided. Thus there is a point at which each form of government blends with the next; and we see that, under three denominations only, the government is really susceptible of as many different forms as the state has citizens.

What is more, this same government being in certain respects capable of subdivision into other parts, one administered in one way, another in another, there may result from combinations of these three forms a multitude of mixed forms, each of which can be multiplied by all the simple forms.

In all ages there has been much discussion about the best form of government, without consideration of the fact that each of them is the best in certain cases, and the worst in others.

If, in the different states, the number of the supreme magistrates should be in inverse ratio to that of the citizens, it follows that, in general, democratic government is suitable to small states, aristocracy to those of moderate size, and monarchy to large ones. This rule follows immediately from the principle. But how is it possible to estimate the multitude of circumstances which may furnish exceptions?

CHAPTER 4

Democracy

He that makes the law knows better than anyone how it should be executed and interpreted. It would seem, then, that there could be no better constitution than one in which the executive power is united with the legislative; but it is that very circumstance which makes a democratic government inadequate in certain respects, because things which ought to be distinguished are not, and because the Prince and the sovereign, being the same person, only form as it were a government without government.

It is not expedient that he who makes the laws should execute them, nor that the body of the people should divert its attention from general considerations in order to bestow it on particular objects. Nothing is more dangerous than the influence of his private interests on public affairs; and the abuse of the laws by the government is a less evil than the corruption of the legislator, which is the infallible result of the pursuit of private interests. For when the state is changed in its substance all reform becomes impossible. A people which would never abuse the government would likewise never abuse its independence; a people which always governed well would not need to be governed.

Taking the term in its strict sense, there never has existed, and never will exist, any true democracy. It is contrary to the natural order that the majority should govern and that the minority should be governed. It is impossible to imagine that the people should remain in perpetual assembly to attend to public affairs, and it is easily apparent that commissions could not be established for that purpose without the form of administration being changed.

In fact, I think I can lay down as a principle that when the functions of government are shared among several magistracies, the least numerous acquire, sooner or later, the greatest authority, if only on account of the facility in transacting business which naturally leads them on to that.

Moreover, how many things difficult to combine does not this government presuppose! First, a very small state, in which the people may be readily assembled, and in which every citizen can easily know all the rest; secondly, great simplicity of manners, which prevents a multiplicity of affairs and thorny discussions; next, considerable equality in rank and fortune, without which equality in rights and authority could not long subsist; lastly, little or no luxury, for luxury is either the effect of wealth or renders it necessary; it corrupts both the rich and the poor, the former by possession, the latter by covetousness; it betrays the country to effeminacy and vanity; it deprives the state of all its citizens in order to subject them one to another, and all to opinion.

That is why a famous author has assigned virtue as the principle of a republic, for all these conditions could not subsist without virtue; but, through not making the necessary distinctions, this brilliant genius has often lacked precision and sometimes clearness, and has not seen that the sovereign authority being everywhere the same, the same principle ought to have a place in every well-constituted state, in a greater or less degree, it is true, according to the form of government.

Let us add that there is no government so subject to civil wars and internal agitations as the democratic or popular, because there is none which tends so strongly and so constantly to change its form, none which demands more vigilance and courage to be maintained in its own form. It is especially in this constitution that the citizen should arm himself with strength and steadfastness, and say every day of his life from the bottom of his heart what a virtuous Palatine* said in the Diet of Poland: *Malo periculosam libertatem quam quietum servitium.*[1]

If there were a nation of gods, it would be governed democratically. So perfect a government is unsuited to men.

---

* The Palatine of Posnania, father of the King of Poland, Duke of Lorraine.
[1] ['I prefer a perilous freedom to a peaceful slavery.']

CHAPTER 5

Aristocracy

We have here two moral persons quite distinct, *viz.* the government and the sovereign; and consequently two general wills, the one having reference to all the citizens, the other only to the members of the administration. Thus, although the government can regulate its internal policy as it pleases, it can never speak to the people except in the name of the sovereign, that is, in the name of the people themselves. This must never be forgotten.

The earliest societies were aristocratically governed. The heads of families deliberated among themselves about public affairs. The young men yielded readily to the authority of experience. Hence the names *priests*, *elders*, *senate*, *gerontes*. The savages of North America are still governed in this way at the present time, and are very well governed.

But in proportion as the inequality due to institutions prevailed over natural inequality, wealth or power* was preferred to age, and aristocracy became elective. Finally, the power transmitted with the father's property to the children, rendering the families patrician, made the government hereditary, and there were senators only twenty years old.

There are, then, three kinds of aristocracy – natural, elective and hereditary. The first is only suitable for simple nations; the third is the worst of all governments. The second is the best; it is aristocracy properly so-called.

Besides the advantage of the distinction between the two powers, aristocracy has that of the choice of its members; for in a popular government all the citizens are born magistrates; but this

---

* It is clear that the word *optimates* among the ancients did not mean the best, but the most powerful.

one limits them to a small number, and they become magistrates by election only;* a method by which probity, intelligence, experience, and all other grounds of preference and public esteem are so many fresh guarantees that men will be wisely governed.

Further, assemblies are more easily convoked; affairs are better discussed and are despatched with greater order and diligence; while the credit of the state is better maintained abroad by venerable senators, than by an unknown or despised multitude.

In a word, it is the best and most natural order of things that the wisest should govern the multitude, when we are sure that they will govern it for its advantage and not for their own. We should not uselessly multiply means, nor do with twenty thousand men what a hundred chosen men can do still better. But we must observe that the corporate interest begins here to direct the public force in a less degree according to the rule of the general will, and that another inevitable propensity deprives the laws of a part of the executive power.

With regard to special expediencies, a state must not be so small, nor a people so simple and upright, that the execution of the laws should follow immediately upon the public will, as in a good democracy. Nor again must a nation be so large that the chief men, who are dispersed in order to govern it, can set up as sovereigns, each in his own province, and begin by making themselves independent so as at last to become masters.

But if aristocracy requires a few virtues less than popular government, it requires also others that are peculiarly its own, such as moderation among the rich and contentment among the poor; for a rigorous equality would seem to be out of place in it, and was not even observed in Sparta.

Besides, if this form of government comports with a certain inequality of fortune, it is expedient in general that the administration of public affairs should be entrusted to those that are best

---

* It is very important to regulate by law the form of election of magistrates; for, in leaving it to the will of the Prince, it is impossible to avoid falling into hereditary aristocracy, as happened in the republics of Venice and Berne. In consequence, the first has long been a decaying state, but the second is maintained by the extreme wisdom of its Senate; it is a very honourable and a very dangerous exception.

able to devote their whole time to it, but not, as Aristotle maintains, that the rich should always be preferred. On the contrary, it is important that an opposite choice should sometimes teach the people that there are, in men's personal merits, reasons for preference more important than wealth.

CHAPTER 6

Monarchy

We have hitherto considered the Prince as a moral and collective person united by the force of the laws, and as the depositary of the executive power in the state. We have now to consider this power concentrated in the hands of a natural person, of a real man, who alone has a right to dispose of it according to the laws. He is what is called a monarch or a king.

Quite the reverse of the other forms of administration, in which a collective being represents an individual, in this one an individual represents a collective being: so that the moral unity that constitutes it is at the same time a physical unity, in which all the powers that the law combines in the other with so much effort are combined naturally.

Thus the will of the people, the will of the Prince, the public force of the state, and the particular force of the government, all obey the same motive power; all the springs of the machine are in the same hand, everything works for the same end; there are no opposite movements that counteract one another, and no kind of constitution can be imagined in which a more considerable action is produced with less effort. Archimedes, quietly seated on the shore, and launching without difficulty a large vessel, represents to me a skilful monarch, governing from his cabinet his vast states, and, while he appears motionless, setting everything in motion.

But if there is no government which has more vigour, there is none in which the particular will has more sway and more easily governs others. Everything works for the same end, it is true; but this end is not the public welfare, and the very power of the administration turns continually to the prejudice of the state.

Kings wish to be absolute, and from afar men cry to them that the best way to become so is to make themselves beloved by their people. This maxim is very fine, and also very true in certain respects; unfortunately it will always be ridiculed in courts. Power which springs from the affections of the people is doubtless the greatest, but it is precarious and conditional; princes will never be satisfied with it. The best kings wish to have the power of being wicked if they please, without ceasing to be masters. A political preacher will tell them in vain that, the strength of the people being their own, it is their greatest interest that the people should be flourishing, numerous, and formidable; they know very well that that is not true. Their personal interest is, in the first place, that the people should be weak and miserable, and should never be able to resist them. Supposing all the subjects always perfectly submissive, I admit that it would then be the prince's interest that the people should be powerful, in order that this power, being his own, might render him formidable to his neighbours; but as this interest is only secondary and subordinate, and as the two suppositions are incompatible, it is natural that princes should always give preference to the maxim which is most immediately useful to them. It is this that Samuel strongly represented to the Hebrews; it is this that Machiavelli clearly demonstrated. While pretending to give lessons to kings, he gave great ones to peoples. The *Prince* of Machiavelli is the book of republicans.*

We have found, by general considerations, that monarchy is suited only to large states; and we shall find this again by examining monarchy itself. The more numerous the public administrative body is, the more does the ratio of the Prince to the subjects diminish and approach equality, so that this ratio is unity or equality, even in a democracy. This same ratio increases in proportion as the government contracts, and is at its maximum when the government is in the hands of a single person. Then the distance between the Prince and the people is too great, and the state lacks cohesion. In

---

* Machiavelli was an honourable man and a good citizen; but, attached to the house of the Medici, he was forced, during the oppression of his country, to conceal his love for liberty. The mere choice of his execrable hero sufficiently manifests his secret intention; and the opposition between the maxims of his book the *Prince* and those of his *Discourses on Titus Livius* and his *History of Florence* shows that this profound politician has had hitherto only superficial or corrupt readers. The court of Rome has strictly prohibited his book; I certainly believe it, for it is that court which he most clearly depicts.

order to unify it, then, intermediate orders, princes, grandees, and nobles, are required to fill them. Now, nothing at all of this kind is proper for a small state, which would be ruined by all these orders.

But if it is difficult for a great state to be well governed, it is much more so for it to be well governed by a single man; and everyone knows what happens when the king appoints deputies.

One essential and inevitable defect, which will always render a monarchical government inferior to a republican one, is that in the latter the public voice hardly ever raises to the highest posts any but enlightened and capable men, who fill them honourably; whereas those who succeed in monarchies are most frequently only petty mischief-makers, petty knaves, petty intriguers, whose petty talents, which enable them to attain high posts in courts, only serve to show the public their ineptitude as soon as they have attained them. The people are much less mistaken about their choice than the prince is; and a man of real merit is almost as rare in a royal ministry as a fool at the head of a republican government. Therefore, when by some fortunate chance one of these born rulers takes the helm of affairs in a monarchy almost wrecked by such a fine set of ministers, it is quite astonishing what resources he finds, and his accession to power forms an epoch in a country.

In order that a monarchical state might be well governed, it would be necessary that its greatness or extent should be proportioned to the abilities of him that governs. It is easier to conquer than to rule. With a sufficient lever, the world may be moved by a finger; but to support it the shoulders of Hercules are required. However small a state may be, the prince is almost always too small for it. When, on the contrary, it happens that the state is too small for its chief, which is very rare, it is still badly governed, because the chief, always pursuing his own great designs, forgets the interests of the people, and renders them no less unhappy by the abuse of his transcendent abilities, than an inferior chief by his lack of talent. It would be necessary, so to speak, that a kingdom should be enlarged or contracted in every reign, according to the capacity of the prince; whereas, the talents of a senate having more definite limits, the state may have permanent boundaries, and the administration prosper equally well.

The most obvious inconvenience of the government of a single person is the lack of that uninterrupted succession which forms in the two others a continuous connection. One king being dead, another is necessary; elections leave dangerous intervals; they are stormy; and unless the citizens are of a disinterestedness, an integrity, which this government hardly admits of, intrigue and corruption intermingle with it. It would be hard for a man to whom the state has been sold not to sell it in his turn, and indemnify himself out of the helpless for the money which the powerful have extorted from him. Sooner or later everything becomes venal under such an administration, and the peace which is then enjoyed under a king is worse than the disorder of an interregnum.

What has been done to prevent these evils? Crowns have been made hereditary in certain families; and an order of succession has been established which prevents any dispute on the demise of kings; that is to say, the inconvenience of regencies being substituted for that of elections, an appearance of tranquillity has been preferred to a wise administration, and men have preferred to risk having as their chiefs children, monsters, and imbeciles, rather than have a dispute about the choice of good kings. They have not considered that in thus exposing themselves to the risk of this alternative, they put almost all the chances against themselves. That was a very sensible answer of Dionysius the younger, to whom his father, in reproaching him with a dishonourable action, said: 'Have I set you the example in this?' 'Ah!' replied the son, 'your father was not a king.'

All things conspire to deprive of justice and reason a man brought up to govern others. Much trouble is taken, so it is said, to teach young princes the art of reigning; this education does not appear to profit them. It would be better to begin by teaching them the art of obeying. The greatest kings that history has celebrated were not trained to rule; that is a science which men are never less masters of than after excessive study of it, and it is better acquired by obeying than by ruling. *Nam utilissimus idem ac brevissimus bonarum malarumque rerum delectus, cogitare quid aut nolueris sub alio principe, aut volueris.*[1]

A result of this want of cohesion is the instability of royal government, which, being regulated sometimes on one plan, sometimes on another, according to the character of the reigning

[1] ['For the quickest and most useful way of choosing between things that are good and evil is to consider what, under another emperor, you would have approved or disapproved.' Tacitus, *Histories* I, 16]

prince or that of the persons who reign for him, cannot long pursue a fixed aim or a consistent course of conduct, a variableness which always makes the state fluctuate between maxim and maxim, project and project, and which does not exist in other governments, where the Prince is always the same. So we see that, in general, if there is more cunning in a court, there is more wisdom in a senate, and that republics pursue their ends by more steadfast and regular methods; whereas every revolution in a royal ministry produces one in the state, the maxim common to all ministers, and to almost all kings, being to reverse in every respect the acts of their predecessors.

From this same want of cohesion is obtained the solution of a sophism very familiar to royal politicians; this is not only to compare civil government with domestic government, and the prince with the father of a family, an error already refuted, but, further, to ascribe freely to this magistrate all the virtues which he might have occasion for, and always to suppose that the prince is what he ought to be – on which supposition royal government is manifestly preferable to every other, because it is incontestably the strongest, and because it only lacks a corporate will more conformable to the general will to be also the best.

But if, according to Plato, a king by nature is so rare a personage, how many times will nature and fortune conspire to crown him? And if the royal education necessarily corrupts those who receive it, what should be expected from a succession of men trained to rule? It is, then, voluntary self-deception to confuse royal government with that of a good king. To see what this government is in itself; we must consider it under incapable or wicked princes; for such will come to the throne, or the throne will make them such.

These difficulties have not escaped our authors, but they have not been embarrassed by them. The remedy, they say, is to obey without murmuring; God gives bad kings in his wrath, and we must endure them as chastisements of heaven. Such talk is doubtless edifying, but I am inclined to think it would be more appropriate in a pulpit than in a book on politics. What should we say of a physician who promises miracles, and whose whole art consists in exhorting the sick man to be patient? We know well that when we have a bad government it must be endured; the question is to find a good one.

CHAPTER 7

Mixed Governments

Properly speaking, there is no simple government. A single chief must have subordinate magistrates; a popular government must have a head. Thus, in the partition of the executive power there is always a gradation from the greater number to the less, with this difference, that sometimes the majority depends on the minority, and sometimes the minority on the majority.

Sometimes there is an equal division, either when the constituent parts are in mutual dependence, as in the government of England; or when the authority of each part is independent, but imperfect, as in Poland. This latter form is bad, because there is no unity in the government, and the state lacks cohesion.

Is a simple or a mixed government the better? A question much debated among publicists, and one to which the same answer must be made that I have before made about every form of government.

The simple government is the better in itself, for the reason that it is simple. But when the executive power is not sufficiently dependent on the legislative, that is, when there is a greater proportion between the Prince and the sovereign than between the people and the Prince, this want of proportion must be remedied by dividing the government; for then all its parts have no less authority over the subjects, and their division renders them all together less strong against the sovereign.

The same inconvenience is also provided against by the establishment of intermediate magistrates, who, leaving the government in its entirety, only serve to balance the two powers and maintain their respective rights. Then the government is not mixed, but temperate.

The opposite inconvenience can be remedied by similar means, and, when the government is too lax, tribunals may be erected to concentrate it. That is customary in all democracies. In the first case the government is divided in order to weaken it, and in the second in order to strengthen it; for the maximum of strength and also of weakness is found in simple governments, while the mixed forms give a medium strength.

That Every Form of Government is Not Fit for Every Country

Liberty, not being a fruit of all climates, is not within the reach of all peoples. The more we consider this principle established by Montesquieu, the more do we perceive its truth; the more it is contested, the greater opportunity is given to establish it by new proofs.

In all the governments of the world, the public person consumes, but produces nothing. Whence, then, comes the substance it consumes? From the labour of its members. It is the superfluity of individuals that supplies the necessaries of the public. Hence it follows that the civil state can subsist only so long as men's labour produces more than they need.

Now this excess is not the same in all countries of the world. In several it is considerable, in others moderate, in others nothing, in others a minus quantity. This proportion depends on the fertility due to climate, on the kind of labour which the soil requires, on the nature of its products, on the physical strength of its inhabitants, on the greater or less consumption that is necessary to them, and on several other like proportions of which it is composed.

On the other hand, all governments are not of the same nature; there are some more or less wasteful; and the differences are based on this other principle, that the further the public contributions are removed from their source, the more burdensome they are. We must not measure this burden by the amount of the imposts, but by the distance they have to traverse in order to return to the hands from which they have come. When this circulation is prompt and well-established, it matters not whether little or much is paid; the people are always rich, and the finances are always prosperous. On the other hand, however little the people may contribute, if this little does not revert to them, they are soon exhausted by constantly giving; the state is never rich and the people are always in beggary.

It follows from this that the more the distance between the people and the government is increased, the more burdensome do the tributes become; therefore, in a democracy the people are least encumbered, in an aristocracy they are more so, and in a monarchy they bear the greatest weight. Monarchy, then, is suited only to wealthy nations; aristocracy, to states moderate both in wealth and size; democracy, to small and poor states.

Indeed, the more we reflect on it, the more do we find in this the difference between free and monarchical states. In the first, everything is used for the common advantage; In the others, public and private resources are reciprocal, and the former are increased by the diminution of the latter; lastly, instead of governing subjects in order to make them happy, despotism renders them miserable in order to govern them.

There are, then, in every climate natural causes by which we can assign the form of government which is adapted to the nature of the climate, and even say what kind of inhabitants the country should have.

Unfruitful and barren places, where the produce does not repay the labour, ought to remain uncultivated and deserted, or should only be peopled by savages; places where men's toil yields only bare necessaries ought to be inhabited by barbarous nations; in them any polity would be an impossibility. Places where the excess of the produce over the labour is moderate are suitable for free nations; those in which abundant and fertile soil yields much produce for little labour are willing to be governed monarchically, in order that the superfluity of the subjects may be consumed by the luxuries of the Prince; for it is better that this excess should be absorbed by the government than squandered by private persons. There are exceptions, I know; but these exceptions themselves confirm the rule, in that, sooner or later, they produce revolutions which restore things to their natural order.

We should always distinguish general laws from the particular causes which may modify their effects. If the whole south should be covered with republics, and the whole north with despotic states, it would not be less true that, through the influence of climate, despotism is suitable to warm countries, barbarism to cold countries, and a good polity to intermediate regions. I see, however, that while the principle is admitted, its application may be disputed; it will be said that some cold countries are very fertile, and some southern ones very unfruitful. But this is a difficulty only for those who do not examine the matter in all its relations. It is necessary, as I have already said, to reckon those connected with labour, resources, consumption, etc.

Let us suppose that the produce of two districts equal in area is in the ratio of five to ten. If the inhabitants of the former consume four and those of the latter nine parts, the surplus produce of the first will be one-fifth, and that of the second one-tenth. The ratio between these two surpluses being then inversely as that of the produce of each, the district which yields only five will give a surplus double that of the district which produces ten.

But it is not a question of double produce, and I do not think that anyone dare, in general, place the fertility of cold countries even on an equality with that of warm countries. Let us, however, assume this equality; let us, if you will, put England in the scales with Sicily, and Poland with Egypt; more to the south we shall have Africa and India; more to the north we shall have nothing. For this equality in produce what a difference in the cultivation! In Sicily it is only necessary to scratch the soil, in England what care is needed to till it! But where more exertion is required to yield the same produce, the surplus must necessarily be very small.

Consider, besides this, that the same number of men consume much less in warm countries. The climate demands that people should be temperate in order to be healthy; Europeans who want to live as at home all die of dysentery and dyspepsia. 'We are,' says Chardin, 'carnivorous beasts, wolves, in comparison with Asiatics. Some attribute the temperance of the Persians to the fact that their country is scantily cultivated; I believe, on the contrary, that their country is not very abundant in provisions because the inhabitants need very little. If their frugality,' he continues, 'resulted from the poverty of the country, it would be only the poor who would eat little, whereas it is the people generally; and more or less would be consumed in each province according to the fertility of the country, whereas the same abstemiousness is found throughout the kingdom. They pride themselves greatly on their mode of living, saying that it is only necessary to look at their complexions, to see how much superior they are to those of Christians. Indeed, the complexions of the Persians are smooth; they have beautiful skins, delicate and clear; while the complexions of their subjects, the Armenians, who live in European fashion, are rough and blotched, and their bodies are coarse and heavy.'

The nearer we approach to the Equator, the less do the people live upon. They eat scarcely any meat; rice, maize, couscous, millet, cassava, are their ordinary foods. There are in India millions of men whose diet does not cost a halfpenny a day. We see even in Europe palpable differences in appetite between northern and southern nations. A Spaniard will live for eight days on a German's dinner. In countries where men are most voracious luxury is directed to matters of consumption; in England it is displayed in a table loaded with meats; in Italy you are regaled with sugar and flowers.

Again, luxury in dress presents similar differences. In climates where the changes of the seasons are sudden and violent, garments are better and simpler; in those where people dress only for ornament, splendour is more sought after than utility, for clothes themselves are a luxury. At Naples you will see men every day walking to Posilippo with gold-embroidered coats, and no stockings. It is the same with regard to buildings; everything is sacrificed to magnificence when there is nothing to fear from injury by the atmosphere. In Paris and in London people must be warmly and comfortably housed; in Madrid they have superb drawing-rooms, but no windows that shut, while they sleep in mere closets.

The foods are much more substantial and nutritious in warm countries; this is a third difference which cannot fail to influence the second. Why do people eat so many vegetables in Italy? Because they are good, nourishing, and of excellent flavour. In France, where they are grown only on water, they are not nourishing and count almost for nothing on the table; they do not, however, occupy less ground, and they cost at least as much labour to cultivate. It is found by experience that the wheats of Barbary, inferior in other respects to those of France, yield much more flour, and that those of France, in their turn, yield more than the wheats of the north. Whence we may infer that a similar gradation is observable generally, in the same direction, from the Equator to the Pole. Now is it not a manifest disadvantage to have in an equal quantity of produce a smaller quantity of nutriment?

To all these different considerations I may add one which springs from, and strengthens, them; it is that warm countries have less need of inhabitants than cold countries, but would be able to maintain a greater number; hence a double surplus is produced, always to the advantage of despotism. The greater the surface occupied by the same number of inhabitants, the more difficult do rebellions become, because measures cannot be concerted promptly and secretly, and because it is always easy for the government to discover the plans and cut off communications. But the more closely packed a numerous population is, the less power has a government to usurp the sovereignty; the chiefs deliberate as securely in their cabinets as the prince in his council, and the multitude assemble in the squares as quickly as the troops in their quarters. The advantage, then, of a tyrannical government lies in this, that it acts at great distances. By help of the points of support which it procures, its power increases with the distance, like that of levers.* That of the people, on the other hand, acts only when concentrated; it evaporates and disappears as it extends, like the effect of powder scattered on the ground, which takes fire only grain by grain. The least populous countries are thus the best adapted for tyranny; wild beasts reign only in deserts.

* This does not contradict what I said before (II, 9) on the inconveniences of large states; for there it was a question of the authority of the government over its members, and here it is a question of its power against its subjects. Its scattered members serve as points of support to it for operating at a distance upon the people, but it has no point of support for acting on its members themselves. Thus, the length of the lever is the cause of its weakness in the one case, and of its strength in the other.

CHAPTER 9

The Marks of a Good Government

When, then, it is asked absolutely which is the best government, an insoluble and likewise indeterminate question is propounded; or, if you will, it has as many correct solutions as there are possible combinations in the absolute and relative positions of the nations.

But if it were asked by what sign it can be known whether a given people is well or ill governed, that would be a different matter, and the question of fact might be determined.

It is, however, not settled, because everyone wishes to decide it in his own way. Subjects extol the public tranquillity, citizens the liberty of individuals; the former prefer security of possessions, the latter, that of persons; the former are of opinion that the best government is the most severe, the latter maintain that it is the mildest; the one party wish that crimes should be punished and the other that they should be prevented; the one party think it well to be feared by their neighbours, the other party prefer to be unacquainted with them; the one party are satisfied when money circulates, the other party demand that the people should have bread. Even though there should be agreement on these and other similar points, would further progress be made? Since moral quantities lack a precise mode of measurement, even if people were in accord about the sign, how could they be so about the valuation of it?

For my part, I am always astonished that people fail to recognise a sign so simple, or that they should have the insincerity not to agree about it. What is the object of political association? It is the preservation and prosperity of its members. And what is the surest sign that they are preserved and prosperous? It is their number and population. Do not, then, go and seek elsewhere for this sign so much discussed. All other things being equal, the government under which, without external aids, without naturalisations, and without colonies, the citizens increase and multiply most, is infallibly the best. That under which a people diminishes and decays is the worst. Statisticians, it is now your business; reckon, measure, compare.*

* On the same principle must be judged the centuries which deserve preference in respect of the prosperity of the human race. Those in which literature and art were seen to flourish have been too much admired, without the secret object of their cultivation being penetrated, without their fatal consequences being considered: *Idque apud imperitos humanitas vocabatur, quum pars servitutis esset.* ['And this was called civilisation by the ignorant, when it was only part of their slavery.' Tacitus, *Agricola*, xxi.] Shall we never detect in the maxims of books the gross self-interest which makes the authors speak? No, whatever they may say, when, notwithstanding its brilliancy, a country is being depopulated, it is untrue that all goes well, and it is not enough that a poet should have an income of 100,000 livres for his epoch to be the best of all. The apparent repose and tranquillity of the chief men must be regarded less than the welfare of nations as a whole, and especially that of the most populous states. Hail lays waste a few cantons, but it rarely causes scarcity. Riots and civil wars greatly startle the chief men; but they do not produce the real misfortunes of nations, which may even be abated, while it is being disputed who shall tyrannise over them. It is from their permanent condition that their real prosperity or calamities spring; when all is left crushed under the yoke, it is then that everything perishes; it is then that the chief men, destroying them at their leisure, *ubi solitudinem faciunt, pacem appellant.* ['while they are creating a desert, they call it peace.' Tacitus, *Agricola*, xxx.] When the broils of the great agitated the kingdom of France, and the coadjutor of Paris carried a poniard in his pocket to the *Parlement*, that did not prevent the French nation from living happily and harmoniously in free and honourable ease. Greece of old flourished in the midst of the most cruel wars; blood flowed there in streams, and the whole country was covered with men. It seemed, said Machiavelli, that amid murders proscriptions, and civil wars, our republic became more powerful; the virtues of its citizens, their manners, their independence, were more effectual in strengthening it than all its dissensions had been in weakening it. A little agitation gives energy to men's minds, and what makes the race truly prosperous is not so much peace as liberty.

CHAPTER 10

The Abuse of the Government and its Tendency to Degenerate

As the particular will acts incessantly against the general will, so the government makes a continual effort against the sovereignty. The more this effort is increased, the more is the constitution altered; and as there is here no other corporate will which, by resisting that of the Prince, may produce equilibrium with it, it must happen sooner or later that the Prince at length oppresses the sovereign and violates the social treaty. Therein is the inherent and inevitable vice which, from the birth of the body politic, tends without intermission to destroy it, just as old age and death at length destroy the human body.

There are two general ways by which a government degenerates, *viz*. when it contracts, or when the state is dissolved.

The government contracts when it passes from the majority to the minority, that is, from democracy to aristocracy, and from aristocracy to royalty. That is its natural tendency.* If it retrograded from the minority to the majority, it might be said to relax; but this inverse progress is impossible.

* The slow formation and the progress of Venice in her lagoons present a notable example of this succession; it is indeed astonishing that, after more than twelve hundred years, the Venetians seem to be still only in the second stage, which began with the *Serrar di Consiglio* in 1198. As for the ancient Doges, with whom they are reproached, whatever the *Squittinio della libertà veneta* may say, it is proved that they were not their sovereigns.

People will not fail to bring forward as an objection to my views the Roman Republic, which followed, it will be said, a course quite contrary, passing from monarchy to aristocracy, and from aristocracy to democracy. I am very far from regarding it in this way.

The first institution of Romulus was a mixed government, which speedily

In reality, the government never changes its form except when its exhausted energy leaves it too weak to preserve itself; and if it becomes still more relaxed as it extends, its force will be annihilated, and it will no longer subsist. We must therefore concentrate the energy as it dwindles; otherwise the state which it sustains will fall into ruin.

The dissolution of the state may occur in two ways.

Firstly, when the Prince no longer administers the state in accordance with the laws; and, secondly, when he usurps the sovereign power. Then a remarkable change takes place – the state, and not the government, contracts; I mean that the state dissolves, and that another is formed within it, which is composed only of the members of the government, and which is to the rest of the people nothing more than their master and their tyrant. So that as soon as

---

degenerated into despotism. From peculiar causes the state perished before its time, as we see a new-born babe die before attaining manhood. The expulsion of the Tarquins was the real epoch of the birth of the Republic. But it did not at first assume a regular form, because, through not abolishing the patrician order, only a half of the work was done. For, in this way, the hereditary aristocracy, which is the worst of legitimate administrations, remaining in conflict with the democracy, the form of the government, always uncertain and fluctuating, was fixed, as Machiavelli has shown, only on the institution of the tribunes; not till then was there a real government and a true democracy. Indeed, the people then were not only sovereign, but also magistrates and judges; the Senate was only a subordinate tribunal for moderating and concentrating the government; and the consuls themselves, although patricians, although chief magistrates, although generals with absolute authority in war, were in Rome only the presidents of the people.

From that time, moreover, the government seemed to follow its natural inclination, and tend strongly to aristocracy. The patriciate abolishing itself as it were, the aristocracy was no longer in the body of patricians as it is at Venice and Genoa, but in the body of the Senate, composed of patricians and plebeians, and also in the body of tribunes when they began to usurp an active power; for words make no difference in things, and when a nation has chiefs to govern for them, whatever name those chiefs bear, they always form an aristocracy.

From the abuses of aristocracy sprang the civil wars and the triumvirate. Sulla, Julius Caesar, Augustus, became in fact real monarchs; and at length, under the despotism of Tiberius, the state was broken up. Roman history, then, does not belie my principle, but confirms it.

the government usurps the sovereignty, the social compact is broken, and all the ordinary citizens, rightfully regaining their natural liberty, are forced, but not morally bound, to obey.

The same thing occurs also when the members of the government usurp separately the power which they ought to exercise only collectively; which is no less a violation of the laws, and occasions still greater disorder. Then there are, so to speak, as many Princes as magistrates; and the state, not less divided than the government, perishes or changes its form.

When the state is broken up, the abuse of the government, whatever it may be, takes the common name of *anarchy*. To distinguish, democracy degenerates into *ochlocracy*, aristocracy into *oligarchy*; I should add that royalty degenerates into *tyranny*; but this last word is equivocal and requires explanation.

In the vulgar sense a tyrant is a king who governs with violence and without regard to justice and the laws. In the strict sense, a tyrant is a private person who arrogates to himself the royal authority without having a right to it. It is in this sense that the Greeks understood the word tyrant; they bestowed it indifferently on good and bad princes whose authority was not legitimate.* Thus *tyrant* and *usurper* are two words perfectly synonymous.

To give different names to different things, I call the usurper of royal authority a *tyrant*, and the usurper of sovereign power a *despot*. The tyrant is he who, contrary to the laws, takes upon himself to govern according to the laws; the despot is he who sets himself above the laws themselves. Thus the tyrant cannot be a despot, but the despot is always a tyrant.

---

* *Omnes enim et habentur et dicuntur tyranni, qui potestate utuntur perpetua in ea civitate quae libertate usa est.* ['For the reputation and name of tyrant belongs to all who exercise perpetual power in a state which has enjoyed freedom.'] (Corn. Nep., *in Miltiad.*, viii.) It is true that Aristotle (*Nic. Eth.,* VIII, x) distinguishes the tyrant from the king, by the circumstance that the former governs for his own benefit, and the latter only for the benefit of his subjects, but besides the fact that, in general, all the Greek authors have taken the word *tyrant* in a different sense, as appears especially from Xenophon's *Hiero*, it would follow from Aristotle's distinction that, since the beginning of the world, not a single king has yet existed.

CHAPTER 11

The Dissolution of the Body Politic

Such is the natural and inevitable tendency of the best constituted governments. If Sparta and Rome have perished, what state can hope to endure for ever? If we wish to form a durable constitution, let us, then, not dream of making it eternal. In order to succeed we must not attempt the impossible, nor flatter ourselves that we are giving to the work of men a stability which human things do not admit of.

The body politic, as well as the human body, begins to die from its birth, and bears in itself the causes of its own destruction. But both may have a constitution more or less robust, and fitted to preserve them a longer or shorter time. The constitution of man is the work of nature; that of the state is the work of art. It does not rest with men to prolong their lives; it does rest with them to prolong that of the state as far as possible by giving it the best constitution practicable. The best constituted will come to an end, but not so soon as another, unless some unforeseen accident brings about its premature destruction.

The principle of political life is in the sovereign authority. The legislative power is the heart of the state; the executive power is its brain, giving movement to all the parts. The brain may be paralysed and yet the individual may live. A man remains an imbecile and lives; but so soon as the heart ceases its functions, the animal dies.

It is not by laws that the state subsists, but by the legislative power. The law of yesterday is not binding today; but tacit consent is presumed from silence, and the sovereign is supposed to confirm continually the laws which it does not abrogate when able to do so. Whatever it has once declared that it wills, it wills always, unless the declaration is revoked.

Why, then, do people show so much respect for ancient laws? It is on account of their antiquity. We must believe that it is only the excellence of the ancient laws which has enabled them to be so long preserved; unless the sovereign had recognised them as constantly salutary, it would have revoked them a thousand times. That is why, far from being weakened, the laws are ever acquiring fresh vigour in every well-constituted state; the prejudice in favour of antiquity renders them more venerable every day; while, wherever laws are weakened as they grow old, this fact proves that there is no longer any legislative power, and that the state no longer lives.

CHAPTER 12

How the Sovereign Authority is Maintained

The sovereign, having no other force than the legislative power, acts only through the laws; and the laws being nothing but authentic acts of the general will, the sovereign can act only when the people are assembled. The people assembled, it will be said: what a chimera! It is a chimera today; but it was not so two thousand years ago. Have men changed their nature?

The limits of the possible in moral things are less narrow than we think; it is our weaknesses, our vices, our prejudices, that contract them. Sordid souls do not believe in great men; vile slaves smile with a mocking air at the word *liberty*.

From what has been done let us consider what can be done. I shall not speak of the ancient republics of Greece; but the Roman Republic was, it seems to me, a great state, and the city of Rome a great city. The last census in Rome showed that there were 400,000 citizens bearing arms, and the last enumeration of the Empire showed more than 4,000,000 citizens, without reckoning subjects, foreigners, women, children, and slaves.

What a difficulty, we might suppose, there would be in assembling frequently the enormous population of the capital and its environs. Yet few weeks passed without the Roman people being assembled, even several times. Not only did they exercise the rights of sovereignty, but a part of the functions of government. They discussed certain affairs and judged certain causes, and in the public assembly the whole people were almost as often magistrates as citizens.

By going back to the early times of nations, we should find that the majority of the ancient governments, even monarchical ones like those of the Macedonians and the Franks, had similar councils. Be that as it may, this single incontestable fact solves all difficulties; inference from the actual to the possible appears to me sound.

CHAPTER 13

How the Sovereign Authority is Maintained
(continued)

It is not sufficient that the assembled people should have once fixed
the constitution of the state by giving their sanction to a body of
laws; it is not sufficient that they should have established a perpetual government, or that they should have once for all provided
for the election of magistrates. Besides the extraordinary assemblies
which unforeseen events may require, it is necessary that there
should be fixed and periodical ones which nothing can abolish or
prorogue; so that, on the appointed day, the people are rightfully
convoked by the law, without needing for that purpose any formal
summons.

But, excepting these assemblies which are lawful by their date
alone, every assembly of the people that has not been convoked by
the magistrates appointed for that duty and according to the
prescribed forms, ought to be regarded as unlawful and all that is
done in it as invalid, because even the order to assemble ought to
emanate from the law.

As for the more or less frequent meetings of the lawful assemblies, they depend on so many considerations that no precise rules
can be given about them. Only it may be said generally that the
more force a government has, the more frequently should the
sovereign display itself.

This, I shall be told, may be good for a single city; but what is to
be done when the state comprises many cities? Will the sovereign
authority be divided? Or must it be concentrated in a single city
and render subject all the rest?

I answer that neither alternative is necessary. In the first place,
the sovereign authority is simple and undivided, and we cannot
divide it without destroying it. In the second place, a city, no more

than a nation, can be lawfully subject to another, because the essence of the body politic consists in the union of obedience and liberty, and these words, *subject* and *sovereign*, are correlatives, the notion underlying them being expressed in the one word *citizen*.

I answer, further, that it is always an evil to combine several towns into a single state, and in desiring to effect such a union we must not flatter ourselves that we shall avoid the natural inconveniences of it. The abuses of great states cannot be brought as an objection against a man who only desires small ones. But how can small states be endowed with sufficient force to resist great ones? Just in the same way as when the Greek towns of old resisted the Great King, and as more recently Holland and Switzerland have resisted the House of Austria.

If, however, the state cannot be reduced to proper limits, one resource still remains; it is not to allow any capital, but to make the government sit alternately in each town, and also to assemble in them by turns the estates of the country.

People the territory uniformly, extend the same rights everywhere, spread everywhere abundance and life: in this way the state will become at once the strongest and the best governed that may be possible. Remember that the walls of the towns are formed solely of the remains of houses in the country. For every palace that I see rising in the capital, I seem to see a whole rural district laid in ruins.

CHAPTER 14

How the Sovereign Authority is Maintained
(continued)

So soon as the people are lawfully assembled as a sovereign body, the whole jurisdiction of the government ceases, the executive power is suspended, and the person of the meanest citizen is as sacred and inviolable as that of the first magistrate, because where the represented are, there is no longer any representative. Most of the tumults that arose in Rome in the *comitia* proceeded from ignorance or neglect of this rule. The consuls were then only presidents of the people and the tribunes simple orators;* the Senate had no power at all.

These intervals of suspension, in which the Prince recognises or ought to recognise the presence of a superior, have always been dreaded by that power; and these assemblies of the people, which are the shield of the body politic and the curb of the government, have in all ages been the terror of the chief men; hence such men are never wanting in solicitude, objections, obstacles, and promises, in the endeavour to make the citizens disgusted with the assemblies. When the latter are avaricious, cowardly, pusillanimous, and more desirous of repose than of freedom, they do not long hold out against the repeated efforts of the government; and thus, as the resisting force constantly increases, the sovereign authority at last disappears, and most of the states decay and perish before their time.

But between the sovereign authority and an arbitrary government there is sometimes introduced an intermediate power of which I must speak.

---

* Almost in the sense given to this term in the Parliament of England. The resemblance between their offices would have set the consuls and tribunes in conflict, even if all jurisdiction had been suspended.

CHAPTER 15

Deputies or Representatives

So soon as the service of the state ceases to be the principal business of the citizens, and they prefer to render aid with their purses rather than their persons, the state is already on the brink of ruin. Is it necessary to march to battle, they pay troops and remain at home; is it necessary to go to the council, they elect deputies and remain at home. As a result of indolence and wealth, they at length have soldiers to enslave their country and representatives to sell it.

It is the bustle of commerce and of the arts, it is the greedy pursuit of gain, it is effeminacy and love of comforts, that commute personal services for money. Men sacrifice a portion of their profit in order to increase it at their ease. Give money and soon you will have chains. That word *finance* is a slave's word; it is unknown among citizens. In a country that is really free, the citizens do everything with their hands and nothing with money; far from paying for exemption from their duties, they would pay to perform them themselves. I am far removed from ordinary ideas; I believe that statute-labour (*les corvées*) is less repugnant to liberty than taxation is.

The better constituted a state is, the more do public affairs outweigh private ones in the minds of the citizens. There is, indeed, a much smaller number of private affairs, because the amount of the general prosperity furnishes a more considerable portion to that of each individual, and less remains to be sought by individual exertions. In a well-conducted city-state everyone hastens to the assemblies; while under a bad government no one cares to move a step in order to attend them, because no one takes an interest in the proceedings, since it is foreseen that the general will will not prevail; and so at last private concerns become all-absorbing. Good laws pave the way for better ones; bad laws lead to worse ones. As soon as anyone says of the affairs of the state, 'Of what importance are they to me?' we must consider that the state is lost.

The decline of patriotism, the active pursuit of private interests, the vast size of states, conquests, and the abuses of government, have suggested the plan of deputies or representatives of the people in the assemblies of the nation. It is this which in certain countries they dare to call the third estate. Thus the private interest of two orders is put in the first and second rank, the public interest only in the third.

Sovereignty cannot be represented for the same reason that it cannot be alienated; it consists essentially in the general will, and the will cannot be represented; it is the same or it is different; there is no medium. The deputies of the people, then, are not and cannot be its representatives; they are only its commissioners and can conclude nothing definitely. Every law which the people in person have not ratified is invalid; it is not a law. The English nation thinks that it is free, but is greatly mistaken, for it is so only during the election of members of Parliament; as soon as they are elected, it is enslaved and counts for nothing. The use which it makes of the brief moments of freedom renders the loss of liberty well-deserved.

The idea of representatives is modern; it comes to us from feudal government, that absurd and iniquitous government, under which mankind is degraded and the name of man dishonoured. In the republics, and even in the monarchies, of antiquity, the people never had representatives; they did not know the word. It is very singular that in Rome, where the tribunes were so sacred, it was not even imagined that they could usurp the functions of the people, and in the midst of so great a multitude, they never attempted to pass of their own accord a single *plebiscitum*. We may judge, however, of the embarrassment which the crowd sometimes caused from what occurred in the time of the Gracchi, when a part of the citizens gave their votes on the house-tops. But where right and liberty are all in all, inconveniences are nothing. In that wise nation everything was estimated at a true value; it allowed the lictors to do what the tribunes had not dared to do, and was not afraid that the lictors would want to represent it.

To explain, however, in what manner the tribunes sometimes

represented it, it is sufficient to understand how the government represents the sovereign. The law being nothing but the declaration of the general will, it is clear that in their legislative capacity the people cannot be represented; but they can and should be represented in the executive power, which is only force applied to law. This shows that very few nations would, upon careful examination, be found to have laws. Be that as it may, it is certain that the tribunes, having no share in the executive power, could never represent the Roman people by right of their office, but only by encroaching on the rights of the Senate.

Among the Greeks, whatever the people had to do, they did themselves; they were constantly assembled in the public place. They lived in a mild climate and they were not avaricious; slaves performed the manual labour; the people's great business was liberty. Not having the same advantages, how are you to preserve the same rights? Your more rigorous climates give you more wants;* for six months in a year the public place is untenable, and your hoarse voices cannot be heard in the open air. You care more for gain than for liberty, and you fear slavery far less than you do misery.

What! is liberty maintained only with the help of slavery? Perhaps; extremes meet. Everything which is not according to nature has its inconveniences, and civil society more than all the rest. There are circumstances so unfortunate that people can preserve their freedom only at the expense of that of others, and the citizen cannot be completely free except when the slave is enslaved to the utmost. Such was the position of Sparta. As for you, modern nations, you have no slaves, but you are slaves; you pay for their freedom with your own. In vain do you boast of this preference; I find in it more of cowardice than of humanity.

I do not mean by all this that slaves are necessary and that the right of slavery is lawful, since I have proved the contrary; I only mention the reasons why modern nations who believe themselves free have representatives, and why ancient nations had none. Be that as it may, as soon as a nation appoints representatives, it is no longer free; it no longer exists.

---

* To adopt in cold countries the effeminacy and luxuriousness of Orientals is to be willing to assume their chains, and to submit to them even more necessarily than they do.

After very careful consideration I do not see that it is possible henceforward for the sovereign to preserve among us the exercise of its rights unless the state is very small. But if it is very small will it not be subjugated? No; I shall show hereafter* how the external power of a great nation can be combined with the convenient polity and good order of a small state.

---

* It is this which I had intended to do in the sequel to this work, when, in treating of external relations, I came to confederations – a wholly new subject, the principles of which have yet to be established.

CHAPTER 16

That the Institution of the Government is Not a Contract

The legislative power being once well established, the question is to establish also the executive power; for this latter, which operates only by particular acts, not being of the essence of the other, is naturally separated from it. If it were possible that the sovereign, considered as such, should have the executive power, law and fact would be so confounded that it could no longer be known what is law and what is not; and the body politic, thus perverted, would soon become a prey to the violence against which it was instituted.

The citizens being all equal by the social contract, all can prescribe what all ought to do, while no one has a right to demand that another should do what he will not do himself. Now, it is properly this right, indispensable to make the body politic live and move, which the sovereign gives to the Prince in establishing the government.

Several have pretended that the instrument in this establishment is a contract between the people and the chiefs whom they set over themselves – a contract by which it is stipulated between the two parties on what conditions the one binds itself to rule, the other to obey. It will be agreed, I am sure, that this is a strange method of contracting. But let us see whether such a position is tenable.

First, the supreme authority can no more be modified than alienated; to limit it is to destroy it. It is absurd and contradictory that the sovereign should acknowledge a superior; to bind itself to obey a master is to regain full liberty.

Further, it is evident that this contract of the people with such or such persons is a particular act; whence it follows that the contract cannot be a law nor an act of sovereignty, and that consequently it is unlawful.

Moreover, we see that the contracting parties themselves would be under the law of nature alone, and without any security for the performance of their reciprocal engagements, which is in every way repugnant to the civil state. He who possesses the power being always capable of executing it, we might as well give the name contract to the act of a man who should say to another: 'I give you all my property, on condition that you restore me what you please.'

There is but one contract in the state – that of association; and this of itself excludes any other. No public contract can be conceived which would not be a violation of the first.

CHAPTER 17

The Institution of the Government

Under what general notion, then, must be included the act by which the government is instituted? I shall observe first that this act is complex, or composed of two others, *viz*. the establishment of the law and the execution of the law.

By the first, the sovereign determines that there shall be a governing body established in such or such a form; and it is clear that this act is a law.

By the second, the people nominate the chiefs who will be entrusted with the government when established. Now, this nomination, being a particular act, is not a second law, but only a consequence of the first, and a function of the government.

The difficulty is to understand how there can be an act of government before the government exists, and how the people, who are only sovereign or subjects, can, in certain circumstances, become the Prince or the magistrates.

Here, however, is disclosed one of those astonishing properties of the body politic, by which it reconciles operations apparently contradictory; for this is effected by a sudden conversion of sovereignty into democracy in such a manner that, without any perceptible change, and merely by a new relation of all to all, the citizens, having become magistrates, pass from general acts to particular acts, and from the law to the execution of it.

This change of relation is not a subtlety of speculation without example in practice; it occurs every day in the Parliament of England, in which the Lower House on certain occasions resolves itself into Grand Committee in order to discuss business better, and thus becomes a simple commission instead of the sovereign court that it was the moment before. In this way it afterwards reports to itself, as the House of Commons, what it has just decided in Grand Committee.

Such is the advantage peculiar to a democratic government, that it can be established in fact by a simple act of the general will; and after this, the provisional government remains in power, should that be the form adopted, or establishes in the name of the sovereign the government prescribed by the law; and thus everything is according to rule. It is impossible to institute the government in any other way that is legitimate without renouncing the principles heretofore established.

CHAPTER 18

Means of Preventing Usurpations of the Government

From these explanations it follows, in confirmation of chapter 16, that the act which institutes the government is not a contract, but a law; that the depositaries of the executive power are not the masters of the people, but its officers; that the people can appoint them and dismiss them at pleasure; that for them it is not a question of contracting, but of obeying, and that in undertaking the functions which the state imposes on them, they simply fulfil their duty as citizens, without having in any way a right to discuss the conditions.

When, therefore, it happens that the people institute a hereditary government, whether monarchical in a family or aristocratic in one order of citizens, it is not an engagement that they make, but a provisional form which they give to the administration, until they please to regulate it differently.

It is true that such changes are always dangerous, and that the established government must never be touched except when it becomes incompatible with the public good; but this circumspection is a maxim of policy, not a rule of right; and the state is no more bound to leave the civil authority to its chief men than the military authority to its generals.

Moreover, it is true that in such a case all the formalities requisite to distinguish a regular and lawful act from a seditious tumult, and the will of a whole people from the clamours of a faction, cannot be too carefully observed. It is especially in this case that only such concessions should be made as cannot in strict justice be refused; and from this obligation also the Prince derives a great advantage in preserving its power in spite of the people, without their being able to say that it has usurped the power; for while appearing to exercise nothing but its rights, it may very easily extend them, and, under pretext of maintaining the public peace, obstruct the assemblies designed to re-establish good order; so that it takes advantage of a silence which it prevents from being broken, or of irregularities which it causes to be committed, so as to assume in its favour the approbation of those whom fear renders silent and punish those that dare to speak. It is in this way that the Decemvirs, having at first been elected for one year, and then kept in office for another year, attempted to retain their power in perpetuity by no longer permitting the *comitia* to assemble; and it is by this easy method that all the governments in the world, when once invested with the public force, usurp sooner or later the sovereign authority.

The periodical assemblies of which I have spoken before are fitted to prevent or postpone this evil, especially when they need no formal convocation; for then the Prince cannot interfere with them, without openly proclaiming itself a violator of the laws and an enemy of the state.

These assemblies, which have as their object the maintenance of the social treaty, ought always to be opened with two propositions, which no one should be able to suppress, and which should pass separately by vote.

The first: 'Whether it pleases the sovereign to maintain the present form of government.'

The second: 'Whether it pleases the people to leave the administration to those at present entrusted with it.'

I presuppose here what I believe that I have proved, *viz.* that there is in the state no fundamental law which cannot be revoked, not even the social compact; for if all the citizens assembled in order to break this compact by a solemn agreement, no one can doubt that it would be quite legitimately broken. Grotius even thinks that each man can renounce the state of which he is a member, and regain his natural freedom and his property by quitting the country.* Now it would be absurd if all the citizens combined should be unable to do what each of them can do separately.

---

* It must be clearly understood that no one should leave in order to evade his duty and relieve himself from serving his country at a moment when it needs him. Flight in that case would be criminal and punishable; it would no longer be retirement, but desertion.

BOOK FOUR

CHAPTER 1

That the General Will is Indestructible

So long as a number of men in combination are considered as a single body, they have but one will, which relates to the common preservation and to the general well-being. In such a case all the forces of the state are vigorous and simple, and its principles are clear and luminous; it has no confused and conflicting interests, the common good is everywhere plainly manifest and only good sense is required to perceive it. Peace, union, and equality are foes to political subtleties. Upright and simple-minded men are hard to deceive because of their simplicity; allurements and refined pretexts do not impose upon them; they are not even cunning enough to be dupes. When, in the happiest nation in the world, we see troops of peasants regulating the affairs of the state under an oak and always acting wisely, can we refrain from despising the refinements of other nations, who make themselves illustrious and wretched with so much art and mystery?

A state thus governed needs very few laws; and in so far as it becomes necessary to promulgate new ones, this necessity is universally recognised. The first man to propose them only gives expression to what all have previously felt, and neither factions nor eloquence will be needed to pass into law what everyone has already resolved to do, so soon as he is sure that the rest will act as he does.

What deceives reasoners is that, seeing only states that are ill-constituted from the beginning, they are impressed with the impossibility of maintaining such a policy in those states; they laugh to think of all the follies to which a cunning knave, an insinuating speaker, can persuade the people of Paris or London. They know not that Cromwell would have been put in irons by the people of Berne, and the Duke of Beaufort imprisoned by the Genevese.

But when the social bond begins to be relaxed and the state weakened, when private interests begin to make themselves felt and small associations to exercise influence on the state, the common interest is injuriously affected and finds adversaries; unanimity no longer reigns in the voting; the general will is no longer the will of all; opposition and disputes arise, and the best counsel does not pass uncontested.

Lastly, when the state, on the verge of ruin, no longer subsists except in a vain and illusory form, when the social bond is broken in all hearts, when the basest interest shelters itself impudently under the sacred name of the public welfare, the general will becomes dumb; all, under the guidance of secret motives, no more express their opinions as citizens than if the state had never existed; and, under the name of laws, they deceitfully pass unjust decrees which have only private interest as their end.

Does it follow from this that the general will is destroyed or corrupted? No; it is always constant, unalterable, and pure; but it is subordinated to others which get the better of it. Each detaching his own interest from the common interest, sees clearly that he cannot completely separate it; but his share in the injury done to the state appears to him as nothing in comparison with the exclusive advantage which he aims at appropriating to himself. This particular advantage being excepted, he desires the general welfare for his own interests quite as strongly as any other. Even in selling his vote for money, he does not extinguish in himself the general will, but eludes it. The fault that he commits is to change the state of the question, and to answer something different from what he was asked; so that, instead of saying by a vote: 'It is beneficial to the state', he says: 'It is beneficial to a certain man or a certain party that such or such a motion should pass.' Thus the law of public order in assemblies is not so much to maintain in them the general will as to ensure that it shall always be consulted and always respond.

I might in this place make many reflections on the simple right of voting in every act of sovereignty – a right which nothing can take away from the citizens – and on that of speaking, proposing, dividing, and discussing, which the government is always very careful to leave to its members only; but this important matter would require a separate treatise, and I cannot say everything in this one.

CHAPTER 2

Voting

We see from the previous chapter that the manner in which public affairs are managed may give a sufficiently trustworthy indication of the character and health of the body politic. The more that harmony reigns in the assemblies, that is, the more the voting approaches unanimity, the more also is the general will predominant; but long discussions, dissensions, and uproar proclaim the ascendency of private interests and the decline of the state.

This is not so clearly apparent when two or more orders enter into its constitution, as, in Rome, the patricians and plebeians, whose quarrels often disturbed the *comitia*, even in the palmiest days of the Republic; but this exception is more apparent than real, for, at that time, by a vice inherent in the body politic, there were, so to speak, two states in one; what is not true of the two together is true of each separately. And, indeed, even in the most stormy times, the *plebiscita* of the people, when the Senate did not interfere with them, always passed peaceably and by a large majority of votes; the citizens having but one interest, the people had but one will.

At the other extremity of the circle unanimity returns; that is, when the citizens, fallen into slavery, have no longer either liberty or will. Then fear and flattery change votes into acclamations; men no longer deliberate, but adore or curse. Such was the disgraceful mode of speaking in the Senate under the Emperors. Sometimes it was done with ridiculous precautions. Tacitus observes that under Otho the senators, in overwhelming Vitellius with execrations, affected to make at the same time a frightful noise, in order that, if he happened to become master, he might not know what each of them had said.

From these different considerations are deduced the principles by which we should regulate the method of counting votes and of comparing opinions, according as the general will is more or less easy to ascertain and the state more or less degenerate.

There is but one law which by its nature requires unanimous consent, that is, the social compact; for civil association is the most voluntary act in the world; every man being born free and master of himself, no one can, under any pretext whatever, enslave him without his assent. To decide that the son of a slave is born a slave is to decide that he is not born a man.

If, then, at the time of the social compact, there are opponents of it, their opposition does not invalidate the contract, but only prevents them from being included in it; they are foreigners among citizens. When the state is established, consent lies in residence; to dwell in the territory is to submit to the sovereignty.*

Excepting this original contract, the vote of the majority always binds all the rest, this being a result of the contract itself. But it will be asked how a man can be free and yet forced to conform to wills which are not his own. How are opponents free and yet subject to laws they have not consented to?

I reply that the question is wrongly put. The citizen consents to all the laws, even to those which are passed in spite of him and even to those which punish him when he dares to violate any of them. The unvarying will of all the members of the state is the general will; it is through that that they are citizens and free.† When a law is proposed in the assembly of the people, what is asked of them is not exactly whether they approve the proposition or reject it, but whether it is conformable or not to the general will, which is their own; each one in giving his vote expresses his opinion thereupon; and from the counting of the votes is obtained the declaration of the general will. When, therefore, the opinion opposed to my own

* This must always be understood to relate to a free state, for otherwise family, property, want of an asylum, necessity, or violence, may detain an inhabitant in a country against his will; and then his residence alone no longer supposes his consent to the contract or to the violation of it.

† At Genoa we read in front of the prisons and on the fetters of the galley-slaves the word, *Libertas*. This employment of the device is becoming and just. In reality, it is only the malefactors in all states who prevent the citizen from being free. In a country where all such people are in the galleys the most perfect liberty will be enjoyed.

prevails, that simply shows that I was mistaken, and that what I considered to be the general will was not so. Had my private opinion prevailed, I should have done something other than I wished; and in that case I should not have been free.

This supposes, it is true, that all the marks of the general will are still in the majority; when they cease to be so, whatever side we take, there is no longer any liberty.

In showing before how particular wills were substituted for general wills in public resolutions, I have sufficiently indicated the means practicable for preventing this abuse; I will speak of it again hereafter. With regard to the proportional number of votes for declaring this will, I have also laid down the principles according to which it may be determined. The difference of a single vote destroys unanimity; but between unanimity and equality there are many unequal divisions, at each of which this number can be fixed according to the condition and requirements of the body politic.

Two general principles may serve to regulate these proportions: the one, that the more important and weighty the resolutions, the nearer should the opinion which prevails approach unanimity; the other, that the greater the despatch requisite in the matter under discussion, the more should we restrict the prescribed difference in the division of opinions; in resolutions which must be come to immediately the majority of a single vote should suffice. The first of these principles appears more suitable to laws, the second to affairs. Be that as it may, it is by their combination that are established the best proportions which can be assigned for the decision of a majority.

CHAPTER 3

Elections

With regard to the elections of the Prince and the magistrates which are, as I have said, complex acts, there are two modes of procedure, *viz.* choice and lot. Both have been employed in different republics, and a very complicated mixture of the two is seen even now in the election of the Doge of Venice.

'Election by lot,' says Montesquieu, 'is of the nature of democracy.' I agree, but how is it so? 'The lot,' he continues, 'is a mode of election which mortifies no one; it leaves every citizen a reasonable hope of serving his country.' But these are not the reasons.

If we are mindful that the election of the chiefs is a function of government and not of sovereignty, we shall see why the method of election by lot is more in the nature of democracy, in which the administration is by so much the better as its acts are less multiplied.

In every true democracy, the magistracy is not a boon but an onerous charge, which cannot fairly be imposed on one individual rather than on another. The law alone can impose this burden on the person upon whom the lot falls. For then, the conditions being equal for all, and the choice not being dependent on any human will, there is no particular application to alter the universality of the law.

In an aristocracy the Prince chooses the Prince, the government is maintained by itself, and voting is rightly established.

The instance of the election of the Doge of Venice, far from destroying this distinction, confirms it; this composite form is suitable in a mixed government. For it is an error to take the government of Venice as a true aristocracy. If the people have no share in the government, the nobles themselves are numerous. A multitude of poor *Barnabotes* never come near any magistracy, and have for their nobility only the empty title of Excellency and the right to attend the Great Council. This Great Council being as numerous as our General Council at Geneva, its illustrious members have no more privileges than our simple citizens (*citoyens*). It is certain that, setting aside the extreme disparity of the two Republics, the burgesses (*la bourgeoisie*) of Geneva exactly correspond to the Venetian order of patricians; our natives (*natifs*) and residents (*habitants*) represent the citizens and people of Venice; our peasants (*paysans*) represent the subjects of the mainland; in short, in whatever way we consider this Republic apart from its size, its government is no more aristocratic than ours. The whole difference is that, having no chief for life, we have not the same need for election by lot.

Elections by lot would have few drawbacks in a true democracy, in which, all being equal as well in character and ability as in sentiments and fortune, the choice would become almost indifferent. But I have already said that there is no true democracy.

When choice and lot are combined, the first should be employed to fill the posts that require peculiar talents, such as military appointments; the other is suitable for those in which good sense, justice, and integrity are sufficient, such as judicial offices, because, in a well-constituted state, these qualities are common to all the citizens.

Neither lot nor voting has any place in a monarchical government. The monarch being by right sole Prince and sole magistrate, the choice of his lieutenants belongs to him alone. When the Abbé de Saint-Pierre proposed to multiply the councils of the King of France and to elect the members of them by ballot, he did not see that he was proposing to change the form of government.

It would remain for me to speak of the method for recording and collecting votes in the assembly of the people; but perhaps the history of the Roman policy in that respect will explain more clearly all the principles which I might be able to establish. It is not unworthy of a judicious reader to see in some detail how public and private affairs were dealt with in a council of 200,000 men.

CHAPTER 4

The Roman Comitia

We have no very trustworthy records of the early times of Rome: there is even great probability that most of the things which have been handed down are fables,* and, in general, the most instructive part of the annals of nations, which is the history of their institution, is the most defective. Experience every day teaches us from what causes spring the revolutions of empires, but, as nations are no longer in process of formation, we have scarcely anything but conjectures to explain how they have been formed.

The customs which are found established at least testify that these customs had a beginning. Of the traditions that go back to these origins, those which the greatest authorities countenance, and which the strongest reasons confirm, ought to pass as the most undoubted. These are the principles which I have tried to follow in enquiring how the freest and most powerful nation in the world exercised its supreme power.

After the foundation of Rome, the growing republic, that is, the army of the founder, composed of Albans, Sabines, and foreigners, was divided into three classes, which, from this division, took the name of *tribes*. Each of these tribes was subdivided into ten *curiae*, and each *curia* into *decuriae*, at the head of which were placed *curiones* and *decurianes*.

Besides this, a body of one hundred horsemen or knights, called a *centuria*, was drawn from each tribe, whence we see that these divisions, not very necessary in a town, were at first only military.

* The name of *Rome*, which is alleged to be derived from *Romulus*, is Greek and means *force*; the name of *Numa* is also Greek and means *law*. What likelihood is there that the first two kings of that city should have borne at the outset names so clearly related to what they did?

But it seems that an instinct of greatness induced the little town of Rome from the first to adopt a polity suitable to the capital of the world.

From this first division an inconvenience soon resulted; the tribe of the Albans* and that of the Sabines† remaining always in the same condition, while that of the foreigners‡ increased continually through perpetual accessions, the last soon outnumbered the two others. The remedy which Servius found for this dangerous abuse was to change the mode of division, and for the division by races, which he abolished, to substitute another derived from the districts of the city occupied by each tribe. Instead of three tribes he made four, each of which occupied one of the hills of Rome and bore its name. Thus, in remedying the existing inequality, he also prevented it for the future; and in order that this might be a division, not only of localities, but of men, he prohibited the inhabitants of one quarter from removing into another, which prevented the races from being mingled.

He also doubled the three old *centuriae* of cavalry and added twelve others to them, but still under the old names – a simple and judicious means by which he effected a distinction between the body of knights and that of the people, without making the latter murmur.

To these four urban tribes Servius added fifteen others, called rural tribes, because they were formed of inhabitants of the country, divided into so many cantons. Afterwards as many new ones were formed; and the Roman people were at length divided into thirty-five tribes, a number which remained fixed until the close of the Republic.

From this distinction between the urban and the rural tribes resulted an effect worthy of notice, because there is no other instance of it, and because Rome owed to it both the preservation of her manners and the growth of her empire. It might be supposed that the urban tribes soon arrogated to themselves the power and the honours, and were ready to disparage the rural tribes. It was quite the reverse. We know the taste of the old Romans for a

* Ramnenses.
† Tatientes.
‡ Luceres.

country life. This taste they derived from their wise founder, who united with liberty rural and military works, and relegated, so to speak, to the towns arts, trades, intrigue, wealth, and slavery.

Thus every eminent man that Rome had being a dweller in the fields and a tiller of the soil, it was customary to seek in the country only for the defenders of the Republic. This condition, being that of the worthiest patricians, was honoured by everyone; the simple and laborious life of villagers was preferred to the lax and indolent life of the burgesses of Rome; and many who would have been only wretched proletarians in the city became, as labourers in the fields, respected citizens. It is not without reason, said Varro, that our high-minded ancestors established in the village the nursery of those hardy and valiant men who defended them in time of war and sustained them in time of peace. Pliny says positively that the rural tribes were honoured because of the men that composed them, while the worthless whom it was desired to disgrace were transferred as a mark of ignominy into the urban tribes. The Sabine Appius Claudius, having come to settle in Rome, was there loaded with honours and enrolled in a rural tribe, which afterwards took the name of his family. Lastly, all the freedmen entered the urban tribes, never the rural; and during the whole of the Republic there is not a single example of any of these freedmen attaining a magistracy, although they had become citizens.

This maxim was excellent, but was pushed so far that at length a change, and certainly an abuse, in government, resulted from it.

First, the censors, after having long arrogated the right of transferring citizens arbitrarily from one tribe to another, allowed the majority to be enrolled in whichever they pleased – a permission which certainly was in no way advantageous, and took away one of the great resources of the censorship. Further, since the great and powerful all enrolled themselves in the rural tribes, while the freedmen who had become citizens remained with the populace in the urban ones, the tribes in general had no longer any district or territory, but all were so intermingled that it was impossible to distinguish the members of each except by the registers; so that the idea of the word *tribe* passed thus from the real to the personal, or rather became almost a chimera.

Moreover, it came about that the urban tribes, being close at hand, were often the most powerful in the *comitia*, and sold the state to those who stooped to buy the votes of the mob of which they were composed.

With regard to the *curiae*, the founder having formed ten in each tribe, the whole Roman people, at that time enclosed in the walls of the city, consisted of thirty *curiae*, each of which had its temples, its gods, its officers, its priests, and its festivals called *compitalia*, resembling the *paganalia* which the rural tribes had afterwards.

In the new division of Servius, the number thirty being incapable of equal distribution into four tribes, he was unwilling to touch them; and the *curiae*, being independent of the tribes, became another division of the inhabitants of Rome. But there was no question of *curiae* either in the rural tribes or in the people composing them, because the tribes having become a purely civil institution, and another mode of levying troops having been introduced, the military divisions of Romulus were found superfluous. Thus, although every citizen was enrolled in a tribe, it was far from being the case that each was enrolled in a *curia*.

Servius made yet a third division, which had no relation to the two preceding, but became by its effects the most important of all. He distributed the whole Roman people into six classes, which he distinguished, not by the place of residence, nor by the men, but by property; so that the first classes were filled with rich men, the last with poor men, and the intermediate ones with those who enjoyed a moderate fortune. These six classes were subdivided into one hundred and ninety-three other bodies called *centuriae*, and these bodies were so distributed that the first class alone comprised more than a half, and the last formed only one. It thus happened that the class least numerous in men had most *centuriae*, and that the last entire class was counted as only one subdivision, although it alone contained more than a half of the inhabitants of Rome.

In order that the people might not so clearly discern the consequences of this last form, Servius affected to give it a military aspect. He introduced in the second class two *centuriae* of armourers, and two of makers of instruments of war in the fourth; in each class, except the last, he distinguished the young and the old, that is to say, those who were obliged to bear arms, and those who were exempted by law on account of age – a distinction which, more than that of property, gave rise to the necessity of frequently repeating the *census* or enumeration; finally, he required that the assembly should be held in the Campus Martius, and that all who were qualified for service by age should gather there with their arms.

The reason why he did not follow in the last class this same division into seniors and juniors is, that the honour of bearing arms for their country was not granted to the populace of which it was composed; it was necessary to have homes in order to obtain the right of defending them; and out of those innumerable troops of beggars with which the armies of kings nowadays glitter, there is perhaps not one but would have been driven with scorn from a Roman cohort when soldiers were defenders of liberty.

Yet again, there was in the last class a distinction between the *proletarii* and those who were called *capite censi*. The former, not altogether destitute, at least supplied citizens to the state, sometimes even soldiers in pressing need. As for those who had nothing at all and could only be counted by heads, they were regarded as altogether unimportant, and Marius was the first who condescended to enrol them.

Without deciding here whether this third enumeration was good or bad in itself, I think I may affirm that nothing but the simple manners of the early Romans — their disinterestedness, their taste for agriculture, their contempt for commerce and for the ardent pursuit of gain — could have rendered it practicable. In what modern nation would rapacious greed, restlessness of spirit, intrigue, continual changes of residence, and the perpetual revolutions of fortune have allowed such an institution to endure for twenty years without the whole state being subverted? It is, indeed, necessary to observe carefully that morality and the censorship, more powerful than this institution, corrected its imperfections in Rome, and that many a rich man was relegated to the class of the poor for making too much display of his wealth.

From all this we may easily understand why mention is scarcely ever made of more than five classes, although there were really six. The sixth, which furnished neither soldiers to the army, nor voters to the Campus Martius,* and which was almost useless in the Republic, rarely counted as anything.

---

* I say 'to the Campus Martius', because it was there that the *comitia centuriata* assembled; in the two other forms the people assembled in the Forum or elsewhere; and then the *capite censi* had as much influence and authority as the chief citizens.

Such were the different divisions of the Roman people. Let us see now what effect they produced in the assemblies. These assemblies, lawfully convened, were called *comitia*; they were usually held in the Forum of Rome or in the Campus Martius, and were distinguished as *comitia curiata*, *comitia centuriata*, and *comitia tributa*, in accordance with that one of the three forms by which they were regulated. The *comitia curiata* were founded by Romulus, the *comitia centuriata* by Servius, and the *comitia tributa* by the tribunes of the people. No law received sanction, no magistrate was elected, except in the *comitia*; and as there was no citizen who was not enrolled in a *curia*, in a *centuria*, or in a tribe, it follows that no citizen was excluded from the right of voting, and that the Roman people were truly sovereign *de jure* and *de facto*.

In order that the *comitia* might be lawfully assembled, and that what was done in them might have the force of law, three conditions were necessary: the first, that the body or magistrate which convoked them should be invested with the necessary authority for that purpose; the second, that the assembly should be held on one of the days permitted by law; the third, that the auguries should be favourable.

The reason for the first regulation need not be explained; the second is a matter of administration; thus it was not permitted to hold the *comitia* on feast days and market days, when the country people, coming to Rome on business, had no leisure to pass the day in the place of assembly. By the third, the Senate kept in check a proud and turbulent people, and seasonably tempered the ardour of seditious tribunes; but the latter found more than one means of freeing themselves from this constraint.

Laws and the election of chiefs were not the only points submitted for the decision of the *comitia*; the Roman people having usurped the most important functions of government, the fate of Europe may be said to have been determined in their assemblies. This variety of subjects gave scope for the different forms which these assemblies took according to the matters which had to be decided.

To judge of these different forms, it is sufficient to compare them. Romulus, in instituting the *curiae*, desired to restrain the Senate by means of the people, and the people by means of the Senate, while ruling equally over all. He therefore gave the people by this form all the authority of numbers in order to balance that of power and wealth, which he left to the patricians. But, according to the spirit of a monarchy, he left still more advantage to the patricians through the influence of their clients in securing a plurality of votes. This admirable institution of patrons and clients was a masterpiece of policy and humanity, without which the patrician order, so opposed to the spirit of a republic, could not have subsisted. Rome alone has had the honour of giving to the world such a fine institution, from which there never resulted any abuse, and which notwithstanding has never been followed.

Since the form of the assembly of the *curiae* subsisted under the kings down to Servius, and since the reign of the last Tarquin is not considered legitimate, the royal laws were on this account generally distinguished by the name of *leges curiatae*.

Under the Republic the assembly of the *curiae*, always limited to the four urban tribes, and containing only the Roman populace, did not correspond either with the Senate, which was at the head of the patricians, or with the tribunes, who, although plebeians, were at the head of the middle-class citizens. It therefore fell into disrepute; and its degradation was such that its thirty assembled lictors did what the *comitia curiata* ought to have done.

The *comitia centuriata* was so favourable to the aristocracy that we do not at first see why the Senate did not always prevail in the *comitia* which bore that name, and by which the consuls, censors, and other curule magistrates were elected. Indeed, of the one hundred and ninety-three *centuriae* which formed the six classes of the whole Roman people, the first class comprising ninety-eight, and the votes being counted only by *centuriae*, this first class alone outnumbered in votes all the others. When all these *centuriae* were in agreement, the recording of votes was even discontinued; what the minority had decided passed for a decision of the multitude; and we may say that in the *comitia centuriata* affairs were regulated rather by the majority of crowns (*écus*) than of votes.

But this excessive power was moderated in two ways: first, the tribunes usually, and a great number of plebeians always, being in the class of the rich, balanced the influence of the patricians in this first class. The second means consisted in this, that instead of making the *centuriae* vote according to their order, which would have caused the first class to begin always, one of them* was drawn by lot and proceeded alone to the election; after which all the *centuriae*, being summoned on another day according to their rank, renewed the election and usually confirmed it. Thus the power of example was taken away from rank to be given to lot, according to the principle of democracy.

From this practice resulted yet another advantage; the citizens from the country had time, between the two elections, to gain information about the merits of the candidate provisionally chosen, and so record their votes with knowledge of the case. But, under pretence of despatch, this practice came to be abolished and the two elections took place on the same day.

The *comitia tributa* were properly the council of the Roman people. They were convoked only by the tribunes; in them the tribunes were elected and passed their *plebiscita*. Not only had the Senate no status in them – it had not even a right to attend; and, being compelled to obey laws on which they could not vote, the senators were, in this respect, less free than the meanest citizens. This injustice was altogether impolitic, and alone sufficed to invalidate the decrees of a body to which all the citizens were not admitted. If all the patricians had taken part in these *comitia* according to the rights which they had as citizens, having become in that case simple individuals, they would have scarcely influenced a form in which votes were counted by the head, and in which the meanest proletarian had as much power as the Chief of the Senate.

We see, then, that besides the order which resulted from these different divisions for the collection of the votes of so great a people, these divisions were not reduced to forms immaterial in themselves, but that each had results corresponding with the purposes for which it was chosen.

Without entering upon this in greater detail, it follows from the preceding explanations that the *comitia tributa* were more favourable to popular government, and the *comitia centuriata* to aristocracy. With regard to the *comitia curiata*, in which the Roman populace alone formed the majority, as they served only to favour tyranny and evil designs, they deserved to fall into discredit, the seditious

---

* This *centuria*, thus chosen by lot, was called *praerogativa*, because its suffrage was demanded first; hence came the word *prerogative*.

themselves refraining from a means which would too plainly reveal their projects. It is certain that the full majesty of the Roman people was found only in the *comitia centuriata*, which were alone complete, seeing that the rural tribes were absent from the *comitia curiata* and the Senate and the patricians from the *comitia tributa*.

The mode of collecting the votes among the early Romans was as simple as their manners, although still less simple than in Sparta. Each gave his vote with a loud voice, and a recording officer duly registered it; a majority of votes in each tribe determined the suffrage of the tribe; a majority of votes among the tribes determined the suffrage of the people; and so with the *curiae* and *centuriae*. This was a good practice so long as probity prevailed among the citizens and everyone was ashamed to record his vote publicly for an unjust measure or an unworthy man; but when the people were corrupted and votes were bought, it was expedient that they should be given secretly in order to restrain purchasers by distrust and give knaves an opportunity of not being traitors.

I know that Cicero blames this change and attributes to it in part the fall of the Republic. But although I feel the weight which Cicero's authority ought to have in this matter, I cannot adopt his opinion; on the contrary, I think that through not making sufficient changes of this kind, the downfall of the state was hastened. As the regimen of healthy persons is unfit for invalids, so we should not desire to govern a corrupt people by the laws which suit a good nation. Nothing supports this maxim better than the duration of the republic of Venice, only the semblance of which now exists, solely because its laws are suitable to none but worthless men.

Tablets, therefore, were distributed to the citizens by means of which each could vote without his decision being known; new formalities were also established for the collection of tablets, the counting of votes, the comparison of numbers, etc.; but this did not prevent suspicions as to the fidelity of the officers* charged with these duties. At length edicts were framed, the multitude of which proves their uselessness.

Towards the closing years, they were often compelled to resort to extraordinary expedients in order to supply the defects of the laws. Sometimes prodigies were feigned; but this method, which

---

* *Custodes, diribitores, rogatores suffragiorum.*

might impose on the people, did not impose on those who governed them. Sometimes an assembly was hastily summoned before the candidates had had time to canvass. Sometimes a whole sitting was consumed in talking when it was seen that the people having been won over were ready to pass a bad resolution. But at last ambition evaded everything; and it seems incredible that in the midst of so many abuses, this great nation, by favour of its ancient institutions, did not cease to elect magistrates, to pass laws, to judge causes, and to despatch public and private affairs with almost as much facility as the Senate itself could have done.

CHAPTER 5

The Tribuneship

When an exact relation cannot be established among the constituent parts of the state, or when indestructible causes are incessantly changing their relations, a special magistracy is instituted, which is not incorporated with the others, but which replaces each term in its true relation, forming a connection or middle term either between the Prince and the people, or between the Prince and the sovereign, or if necessary between both at once.

This body, which I shall call the *tribuneship*, is the guardian of the laws and of the legislative power. It sometimes serves to protect the sovereign against the government, as the tribunes of the people did in Rome; sometimes to support the government against the people, as the Council of Ten now does in Venice; and sometimes to maintain an equilibrium among all parts, as the ephors did in Sparta.

The tribuneship is not a constituent part of the state, and should have no share in the legislative or in the executive power; but it is in this very circumstance that its own power is greatest; for, while unable to do anything, it can prevent everything. It is more sacred and more venerated, as defender of the laws, than the Prince that executes them and the sovereign that enacts them. This was very clearly seen in Rome, when those proud patricians, who always despised the people as a whole, were forced to bow before a simple officer of the people, who had neither auspices nor jurisdiction.

The tribuneship, wisely moderated, is the strongest support of a good constitution; but if its power be ever so little in excess, it overthrows everything. Weakness is not natural to it; and provided it has some power, it is never less than it should be.

It degenerates into tyranny when it usurps the executive power, of which it is only the moderator, and when it wishes to make the laws which it should only defend. The enormous power of the ephors, which was without danger so long as Sparta preserved her morality, accelerated the corruption when it had begun. The blood of Agis, slain by these tyrants, was avenged by his successor; but the crime and the punishment of the ephors alike hastened the fall of the republic, and, after Cleomenes, Sparta was no longer of any account. Rome, again, perished in the same way; and the excessive power of the tribunes, usurped by degrees, served at last, with the aid of laws framed on behalf of liberty, as a shield for the emperors who destroyed her. As for the Council of Ten in Venice, it is a tribunal of blood, horrible both to the patricians and to the people; and, far from resolutely defending the laws, it has only served since their degradation for striking secret blows which men dare not remark.

The tribuneship, like the government, is weakened by the multiplication of its members. When the tribunes of the Roman people, at first two in number and afterwards five, wished to double this number, the Senate allowed them to do so, being quite sure of controlling some by means of others, which did not fail to happen.

The best means of preventing the usurpations of such a formidable body, a means of which no government has hitherto availed itself, would be, not to make this body permanent, but to fix intervals during which it should remain suspended. These intervals, which should not be long enough to allow abuses time to become established, can be fixed by law in such a manner that it may be easy to shorten them in case of need by means of extra-ordinary commissions.

This method appears to me free from objection, because, as I have said, the tribuneship, forming no part of the constitution, can be removed without detriment; and it seems to me efficacious, because a magistrate newly established does not start with the power that his predecessor had, but with that which the law gives him.

CHAPTER 6

The Dictatorship

The inflexibility of the laws, which prevents them from being adapted to emergencies, may in certain cases render them pernicious, and thereby cause the ruin of the state in a time of crisis. The order and tardiness of the forms require a space of time which circumstances sometimes do not allow. A thousand cases may arise for which the legislator has not provided, and to perceive that everything cannot be foreseen is a very needful kind of foresight.

We must therefore not desire to establish political institutions so firmly as to take away the power of suspending their effects. Even Sparta allowed her laws to sleep.

But only the greatest dangers can outweigh that of changing the public order, and the sacred power of the laws should never be interfered with except when the safety of the country is at stake. In these rare and obvious cases, the public security is provided for by a special act, which entrusts the care of it to the most worthy man. This commission can be conferred in two ways, according to the nature of the danger.

If an increase in the activity of the government suffices to remedy this evil, we may concentrate it in one or two of its members; in that case it is not the authority of the laws which is changed but only the form of their administration. But if the danger is such that the formal process of law is an obstacle to our security, a supreme head is nominated, who may silence all the laws and suspend for a moment the sovereign authority. I such a case the general will is not doubtful, and it is clear that the primary intention of the people is that the state should not perish. In this way the suspension of the legislative power does not involve its abolition; the magistrate who silences it can make it speak; he dominates it without having power to represent it; he can do everything but make laws.

The first method was employed by the Roman Senate when it charged the consuls, by a consecrated formula, to provide for the safety of the Republic. The second was adopted when one of the two consuls nominated a dictator,* a usage of which Alba had furnished the precedent to Rome.

At the beginning of the Republic they very often had recourse to the dictatorship, because the state had not yet a sufficiently firm foundation to be able to maintain itself by the vigour of its constitution alone.

Public morality rendering superfluous at that time many precautions that would have been necessary at another time, there was no fear either that a dictator would abuse his authority or that he would attempt to retain it beyond the term. On the contrary, it seemed that so great a power must be a burden to him who was invested with it, such haste did he make to divest himself of it, as if to take the place of the laws were an office too arduous and too dangerous.

Therefore it is the danger, not of its abuse, but of its degradation, that makes me blame the indiscreet use of this supreme magistracy in early times; for whilst it was freely used at elections, at dedications, and in purely formal matters, there was reason to fear that it would become less formidable in case of need, and that the people would grow accustomed to regard as an empty title that which was only employed in empty ceremonies.

Towards the close of the Republic, the Romans, having become more circumspect, used the dictatorship sparingly with as little reason as they had formerly been prodigal of it. It was easy to see that their fear was ill-founded; that the weakness of the capital then constituted its security against the magistrates whom it had within it; that a dictator could, in certain cases, defend the public liberty without ever being able to assail it; and that the chains of Rome would not be forged in Rome itself, but in her armies. The slight resistance which Marius made against Sulla, and Pompey against Caesar, showed clearly what might be looked for from the authority within against the force without.

---

* This nomination was made by night and in secret, as if they were ashamed to set a man above the laws.

This error caused them to commit great mistakes; such, for example, was that of not appointing a dictator in the Catiline affair; for as it was only a question of the interior of the city, or at most of some province of Italy, a dictator, with the unlimited authority that the laws gave him, would have easily broken up the conspiracy, which was suppressed only by a combination of happy accidents such as human prudence could not have foreseen.

Instead of that, the Senate was content to entrust all its power to the consuls; whence it happened that Cicero, in order to act effectively, was constrained to exceed his authority in a material point, and that, although the first transports of joy caused his conduct to be approved, he was afterwards justly called to account for the blood of citizens shed contrary to the laws, a reproach which could not have been brought against a dictator. But the consul's eloquence won over everybody; and he himself, although a Roman, preferred his own glory to his country's good, and sought not so much the most certain and legitimate means of saving the state as the way to secure the whole credit of this affair.* Therefore he was justly honoured as the liberator of Rome and justly punished as a violator of the laws. However brilliant his recall may have been, it was certainly a pardon.

Moreover, in whatever way this important commission may be conferred, it is important to fix its duration at a very short term which can never be prolonged. In the crises which cause it to be established, the state is soon destroyed or saved; and, the urgent need having passed away, the dictatorship becomes tyrannical or useless. In Rome the dictators held office for six months only, and the majority abdicated before the end of this term. Had the term been longer, they would perhaps have been tempted to prolong it still further, as the Decemvirs did their term of one year. The dictator only had time to provide for the necessity which had led to his election; he had no time to think of other projects.

* He could not be satisfied about this in proposing a dictator; he dared not nominate himself, and could not feel sure that his colleague would nominate him.

CHAPTER 7

The Censorship

Just as the declaration of the general will is made by the law, the declaration of public opinion is made by the censorship. Public opinion is a kind of law of which the censor is minister, and which he only applies to particular cases in the manner of the Prince.

The censorial tribunal, then, far from being the arbiter of the opinion of the people, only declares it, and so soon as it departs from this position, its decisions are fruitless and ineffectual.

It is useless to distinguish the character of a nation from the objects of its esteem, for all these things depend on the same principle and are necessarily intermixed. In all the nations of the world it is not nature but opinion which decides the choice of their pleasures. Reform men's opinions and their manners will be purified of themselves. People always like what is becoming or what they judge to be so; but it is in this judgment that they make mistakes; the question, then, is to guide their judgment. He who judges of manners judges of honour; and he who judges of honour takes his law from opinion.

The opinions of a nation spring from its constitution. Although the law does not regulate morality, it is legislation that gives it birth, and when legislation becomes impaired, morality degenerates; but then the judgment of the censors will not do what the power of the laws has failed to do.

It follows from this that the censorship may be useful to preserve morality, never to restore it. Institute censors while the laws are vigorous; so soon as they have lost their power all is over. Nothing that is lawful has any force when the laws cease to have any.

The censorship supports morality by preventing opinions from being corrupted, by preserving their integrity through wise applications, sometimes even by fixing them when they are still uncertain. The use of seconds in duels, carried to a mad extreme in the kingdom of France, was abolished by these simple words in an edict of the king: 'As for those who have the cowardice to appoint seconds'. This judgment, anticipating that of the public, immediately decided it. But when the same edicts wanted to declare that it was also cowardice to fight a duel, which is very true, but contrary to common opinion, the public ridiculed this decision, on which its judgment was already formed.

I have said elsewhere* that as public opinion is not subject to constraint, there should be no vestige of this in the tribunal established to represent it. We cannot admire too much the art with which this force, wholly lost among the moderns, was set in operation among the Romans and still better among the Lacedaemonians.

A man of bad character having brought forward a good measure in the Council of Sparta, the ephors, without regarding him, caused the same measure to be proposed by a virtuous citizen. What an honour for the one, what a stigma for the other, without praise or blame being given to either! Certain drunkards from Samos† defiled the tribunal of the ephors; on the morrow a public edict granted permission to the Samians to be filthy. A real punishment would have been less severe than such impunity. When Sparta pronounced what was or was not honourable, Greece made no appeal from her decisions.

---

* I merely indicate in this chapter what I have treated at greater length in the *Letter to M. d'Alembert*.

† They were from another island, which the delicacy of our language forbids us to name on this occasion. [The island was Chios.]

CHAPTER 8

Civil Religion

Men had at first no kings except the gods and no government but a theocracy. They reasoned like Caligula, and at that time they reasoned rightly. A long period is needed to change men's sentiments and ideas in order that they may resolve to take a fellow-man as a master and flatter themselves that all will be well.

From the single circumstance that a god was placed at the head of every political society, it followed that there were as many gods as nations. Two nations foreign to each other, and almost always hostile, could not long acknowledge the same master; two armies engaged in battle with each other could not obey the same leader. Thus from national divisions resulted polytheism, and from this, theological and civil intolerance, which are by nature the same, as will be shown hereafter.

The fancy of the Greeks that they recognised their own gods among barbarous nations arose from their regarding themselves as the natural sovereigns of those nations. But in our days that is a very ridiculous kind of erudition which turns on the identity of the gods of different nations, as if Moloch, Saturn, and Chronos could be the same god! As if the Baal of the Phoenicians, the Zeus of the Greeks, and the Jupiter of the Latins could be the same! As if there could be anything in common among imaginary beings bearing different names!

But if it is asked why under paganism, when every state had its worship and its gods, there were no wars of religion, I answer that it was for the same reason that each state, having its peculiar form of worship as well as its own government, did not distinguish its gods from its laws. Political warfare was also religious, the departments of the gods were, so to speak, fixed by the limits of the nations. The god of one nation had no right over other nations.

The gods of the pagans were not jealous gods; they shared among them the empire of the world; even Moses and the Hebrew nation sometimes countenanced this idea by speaking of the god of Israel. It is true that they regarded as nought the gods of the Canaanites, proscribed nations, devoted to destruction, whose country they were to occupy; but see how they spoke of the divinities of the neighbouring nations whom they were forbidden to attack: 'The possession of what belongs to Chamos your god,' said Jephthah to the Ammonites, 'is it not lawfully your due? By the same title we possess the lands which our conquering god has acquired.'* In this, it seems to me, there was a well-recognised parity between the rights of Chamos and those of the god of Israel.

But when the Jews, subjected to the kings of Babylon, and afterwards to the kings of Syria, obstinately refused to acknowledge any other god than their own, this refusal being regarded as a rebellion against the conqueror, drew upon them the persecutions which we read of in their history, and of which no other instance appears before Christianity.†

Every religion, then, being exclusively attached to the laws of the state which prescribed it, there was no other way of converting a nation than to subdue it, and no other missionaries than conquerors; and the obligation to change their form of worship being the law imposed on the vanquished, it was necessary to begin by conquering before speaking of conversions. Far from men fighting or the gods, it was, as in Homer, the gods who fought for men; each sued for victory from his own god and paid for it with new altars. The Romans, before attacking a place, summoned its gods to abandon it; and when they left to the Tarentines their exasperated gods, it was because they then re-

---

* 'Nonne ea quae possidet Chamos deus tuus tibi jure debentur?' (Judges xi, 24). Such is the text of the Vulgate. Père de Carrières has translated it thus: 'Do you not believe that you have a right to possess what belongs to Chamos your god?' I am ignorant of the force of the Hebrew text, but I see that in the Vulgate Jephthah positively acknowledges the right of the god Chamos, and that the French translator weakens this acknowledgment by an 'according to you' which is not in the Latin.

† There is the strongest evidence that the war of the Phocaeans, called a sacred war, was not a war of religion. Its object was to punish sacrilege, and not to subdue unbelievers.

garded these gods as subjected to their own and forced to pay them homage. They left the vanquished their gods as they left them their laws. A crown for the Capitoline Jupiter was often the only tribute that they imposed.

At last, the Romans having extended their worship and their laws with their empire, and having themselves often adopted those of the vanquished, the nations of this vast empire, since the light of citizenship was granted to all, found insensibly that they had multitudes of gods and religions, almost the same everywhere; and this is why paganism was at length known in the world as only a single religion.

It was in these circumstances that Jesus came to establish on earth a spiritual kingdom, which, separating the religious from the political system, destroyed the unity of the state, and caused the intestine divisions which have never ceased to agitate Christian nations. Now this new idea of a kingdom in the other world having never been able to enter the minds of the pagans, they always regarded Christians as actual rebels, who, under cover of a hypocritical submission, only sought an opportunity to make themselves independent and supreme, and to usurp by cunning the authority which, in their weakness, they pretended to respect. This was the cause of persecutions.

What the pagans had feared came to pass. Then everything changed its aspect; the humble Christians altered their tone, and soon this pretended kingdom of the other world became, under a visible chief, the most violent despotism in this world.

As, however, there have always been a Prince and civil laws, a perpetual conflict of jurisdiction has resulted from this double power, which has rendered any good polity impossible in Christian states; and no one has ever succeeded in understanding whether he was bound to obey the ruler or the priest.

Many nations, however, even in Europe or on its outskirts, wished to preserve or to re-establish the ancient system, but without success; the spirit of Christianity prevailed over everything. The sacred worship always retained or regained its independence of the sovereign, and without any necessary connection with the body of the state. Muhammad had very sound views; he thoroughly unified his political system; and so long as his form of government subsisted under his successors, the khalifs, the government was quite undivided and in that respect good. But the Arabs having become flourishing, learned, polished, effeminate, and indolent, were subjugated by the barbarians, and then the division between the two powers began again. Although it may be less apparent among the Muhammadans than among the Christians, the division nevertheless exists, especially in the sect of Ali; and there are states, such as Persia, in which it is still seen.

Among us, the kings of England have established themselves as heads of the church, and the Tsars have done the same; but by means of this title they have made themselves its ministers rather than its rulers; they have acquired not so much the right of changing it as the power of maintaining it; they are not its legislators but only its princes. Wherever the clergy form a corporation,* they are masters and legislators in their own country. There are, then, two powers, two sovereigns, in England and in Russia, just as elsewhere.

Of all Christian authors, the philosopher Hobbes is the only one who has clearly seen the evil and its remedy, and who has dared to propose a reunion of the heads of the eagle and the complete restoration of political unity, without which no state or government will ever be well constituted. But he ought to have seen that the domineering spirit of Christianity was incompatible with his system, and that the interest of the priest would always be stronger than that of the state. It is not so much what is horrible and false in his political theory as what is just and true that has rendered it odious.†

I believe that by developing historical facts from this point of view, the opposite opinions of Bayle and Warburton might easily be

---

* It must, indeed, be remarked that it is not so much the formal assemblies, like those in France, that bind the clergy into one body, as the communion of churches. Communion and excommunication are the social pact of the clergy, a pact by means of which they will always be the masters of nations and kings. All priests who are of the same communion are fellow citizens, though they are as far asunder as the poles. This invention is a masterpiece of policy. There was nothing similar among pagan priests; therefore they never formed a body of clergy.

† See, among others, in a letter from Grotius to his brother of the 11th April, 1643, what that learned man approves and what he blames in the book *De Cive*. It is true that, inclined to indulgence, he appears to pardon the author for the good for the sake of the evil, but everyone is not so merciful.

refuted. The former of these maintains that no religion is useful to the body politic; the latter, on the other hand, asserts that Christianity is its strongest support. To the first it might be proved that no state was ever founded without religion serving as its basis, and to the second, that the Christian law is more injurious than useful to a firm constitution of the state. In order to succeed in making myself understood, I need only give a little more precision to the exceedingly vague ideas about religion in its relation to my subject.

Religion, considered with reference to society, which is either general or particular, may also be divided into two kinds, *viz.* the religion of the man and that of the citizen. The first, without temples, without altars, without rites, limited to the purely internal worship of the supreme God and to the eternal duties of morality, is the pure and simple religion of the Gospel, the true theism, and what may be called the natural divine law. The other, inscribed in a single country, gives to it its gods, its peculiar and tutelary patrons. It has its dogmas, its rites, its external worship prescribed by the laws; outside the single nation which observes it everything is for it infidel, foreign, and barbarous; it extends the duties and rights of men only as far as its altars. Such were all the religions of early nations, to which may be given the name of divine law, civil or positive.

There is a third and more extravagant kind of religion, which, giving to men two sets of laws, two chiefs, two countries, imposes on them contradictory duties, and prevents them from being at once devout men and citizens. Such is the religion of the Lamas, such is that of the Japanese, such is Roman Christianity. This may be called the religion of the priest. There results from it a kind of mixed and unsocial law which has no name.

Considered politically, these three kinds of religion all have their defects. The third is so evidently bad that it would be a waste of time to stop and prove this. Whatever destroys social unity is good for nothing; all institutions which put a man in contradiction with himself are worthless.

The second is good so far as it combines divine worship with love for the laws, and, by making their country the object of the citizens' adoration, teaches them that to serve the state is to serve the guardian deity. It is a kind of theocracy, in which there ought to be no pontiff but the Prince, no other priests than the magistrates.

Then to die for one's country is to suffer martyrdom, to violate the laws is to be impious, and to subject a guilty man to public execration is to devote him to the wrath of the gods: *Sacer esto.*

But it is evil in so far as being based on error and falsehood, it deceives men, renders them credulous and superstitious, and obscures the true worship of the Deity with vain ceremonial. It is evil, again, when, becoming exclusive and tyrannical, it makes a nation sanguinary and intolerant, so that it thirsts after nothing but murder and massacre, and believes that it is performing a holy action in killing whosoever does not acknowledge its gods. This puts such a nation in a natural state of war with all others, which is very prejudicial to its own safety.

There remains, then, the religion of man or Christianity, not that of today, but that of the Gospel, which is quite different. By this holy, sublime, and pure religion, men, children of the same God, all recognise one another as brethren, and the social bond which unites them is not dissolved even at death.

But this religion, having no particular relation with the body politic, leaves to the laws only the force that they derive from themselves, without adding to them any other; and thereby one of the great bonds of the particular society remains ineffective. What is more, far from attaching the hearts of citizens to the state, it detaches them from it and from all earthly things. I know of nothing more contrary to the social spirit.

We are told that a nation of true Christians would form the most perfect society conceivable. In this supposition I see only one great difficulty – that a society of true Christians would be no longer a society of men.

I say even that this supposed society, with all its perfection, would be neither the strongest nor the most durable; by virtue of its perfection it would lack cohesion; its perfection, indeed, would be its destroying vice.

Each man would perform his duty; the people would be obedient to the laws, the chief men would be just and moderate, and the magistrates upright and incorruptible; the soldiers would despise death; there would be neither vanity nor luxury. All this is very good; but let us look further.

Christianity is an entirely spiritual religion, concerned solely with heavenly things; the Christian's country is not of this world.

He does his duty, it is true; but he does it with a profound indifference as to the good or ill success of his endeavours. Provided that he has nothing to reproach himself with, it matters little to him whether all goes well or ill here below. If the state is flourishing, he scarcely dares to enjoy the public felicity; he fears to take a pride in the glory of his country. If the state declines, he blesses the hand of God which lies heavy on his people.

In order that the society might be peaceable and harmony maintained, it would be necessary for all citizens without exception to be equally good Christians; but if unfortunately there happens to be in it a single ambitious man, a single hypocrite, a Catiline or a Cromwell for example, such a man will certainly obtain an advantage over his pious compatriots. Christian charity does not suffer men readily to think ill of their neighbours. As soon as a man has found by cunning the art of imposing on them and securing to himself a share in the public authority, he is invested with dignity; God wills that he should be reverenced. Soon he exercises dominion; God wills that he should be obeyed. The depositary of this power abuses it; this is the rod with which God punishes his children. They would have scruples about driving out the usurper; it would be necessary to disturb the public peace, to employ violence, to shed blood; all this ill accords with the meekness of the Christian, and, after all, does it matter whether they are free or enslaved in this vale of woes? The essential thing is to reach paradise, and resignation is but one means the more towards that.

Some foreign war comes on; the citizens march to battle without anxiety; none of them think of flight. They do their duty, but without an ardent desire for victory; they know better how to die than to conquer. What matters it whether they are the victors or the vanquished? Does not Providence know better than they what is needful for them? Conceive what an advantage a bold, impetuous, enthusiastic enemy can derive from this stoical indifference! Set against them those noble peoples who are consumed with a burning love of glory and of country. Suppose your Christian republic opposed to Sparta or Rome; the pious Christians will be beaten, crushed, destroyed, before they have time to collect themselves, or they will owe their safety only to the contempt which the enemy may conceive for them. To my mind that was a noble oath of the soldiers of Fabius; they did not swear to die or to conquer, they swore to return as conquerors, and kept their oath. Never would Christians have done such a thing; they would have believed that they were tempting God.

But I am mistaken in speaking of a Christian republic; each of these two words excludes the other. Christianity preaches only servitude and dependence. Its spirit is too favourable to tyranny for the latter not to profit by it always. True Christians are made to be slaves; they know it and are hardly aroused by it. This short life has too little value in their eyes.

Christian troops are excellent, we are told. I deny it; let them show me any that are such. For my part, I know of no Christian troops. The crusades will be cited. Without disputing the valour of the crusaders, I shall observe that, far from being Christians, they were soldiers of the priest, citizens of the Church; they fought for their spiritual country, which the Church had somehow rendered temporal. Properly regarded, this brings us back to paganism; as the Gospel does not establish a national religion, any sacred war is impossible among Christians.

Under the pagan emperors Christian soldiers were brave; all Christian authors affirm it, and I believe it. There was a rivalry of honour against the pagan troops. As soon as the emperors became Christians, this rivalry no longer subsisted; and when the cross had driven out the eagle, all the Roman valour disappeared.

But, setting aside political considerations, let us return to the subject of right and determine principles on this important point. The right which the social pact gives to the sovereign over its subjects does not, as I have said, pass the limits of public utility.* Subjects, then, owe no account of their opinions to the sovereign except so far as those opinions are of moment to the community. Now it is very important for the state that every citizen should have a religion which may make him delight in his duties; but the dogmas

---

* 'In the commonwealth,' says the Marquis d'Argenson, 'each is perfectly free in what does not injure others.' That is the unalterable limit; it cannot be more accurately placed. I could not deny myself the pleasure of sometimes quoting this manuscript, although it is not known to the public, in order to do honour to the memory of an illustrious and honourable man, who preserved even in office the heart of a true citizen, and just and sound opinions about the government of his country.

of this religion concern neither the state nor its members, except so far as they affect morality and the duties which he who professes it is bound to perform towards others. Each may have, in addition, such opinions as he pleases, without its being the business of the sovereign to know them; for as he has no jurisdiction in the other world, the destiny of his subjects in the life to come, whatever it may be, is not his affair, provided they are good citizens in this life.

There is, however, a purely civil profession of faith, the articles of which it is the duty of the sovereign to determine, not exactly as dogmas of religion, but as sentiments of sociability, without which it is impossible to be a good citizen or a faithful subject.* Without having power to compel anyone to believe them, the sovereign may banish from the state whoever does not believe them; it may banish him not as impious, but as unsociable, as incapable of sincerely loving law and justice and of sacrificing at need his life to his duty. But if anyone, after publicly acknowledging these dogmas, behaves like an unbeliever in them, he should be punished with death; he has committed the greatest of crimes, he has lied before the laws.

The dogmas of civil religion ought to be simple, few in number, stated with precision, and without explanations or commentaries. The existence of the Deity, powerful, wise, beneficent, prescient, and bountiful, the life to come, the happiness of the just, the punishment of the wicked, the sanctity of the social contract and of the laws; these are the positive dogmas. As for the negative dogmas, I limit them to one only, that is, intolerance; it belongs to the creeds which we have excluded.

Those who distinguish civil intolerance from theological intolerance are, in my opinion, mistaken. These two kinds of intolerance are inseparable. It is impossible to live at peace with people whom we believe to be damned; to love them would be to hate God who punishes them. It is absolutely necessary to reclaim them or to punish them. Wherever theological intolerance is

---

* Caesar, in pleading for Catiline, tried to establish the dogma of the mortality of the soul; Cato and Cicero, to confute him, did not waste time in philosophising; they were content to show that Caesar spoke as a bad citizen and put forward a doctrine pernicious to the state. Indeed, it was that which the Roman Senate had to decide, and not the theological question.

allowed, it cannot but have some effect in civil life;* and as soon as it has any, the sovereign is no longer sovereign even in secular affairs; from that time the priests are the real masters; the kings are only their officers.

Now that there is, and can be, no longer any exclusive national religion, we should tolerate all those which tolerate others, so far as their dogmas have nothing contrary to the duties of a citizen. But whosoever dares to say, 'Outside the Church no salvation', ought to be driven from the state, unless the state be the Church and the Prince be the pontiff. Such a dogma is proper only in a theocratic government; in any other it is pernicious. The reason for which Henry IV is said to have embraced the Romish religion ought to have made any honourable man renounce it, and especially any prince who knew how to reason.

* Marriage, for example, being a civil contract, has civil consequences, without which it is even impossible for society to subsist. Let us, then, suppose that a clergy should succeed in arrogating to itself the sole right to perform this act, a right which it must necessarily usurp in every intolerant religion; then, is it not clear that in taking the opportunity to strengthen the Church's authority, it will render ineffectual that of the Prince, which will no longer have any subjects except those which the clergy are pleased to give it? Having the option of marrying or not marrying people, according as they hold or do not hold such or such a doctrine, according as they admit or reject such or such a formulary, according as they are more or less devoted to it, is it not clear that by behaving prudently and keeping firm, the Church alone will dispose of inheritances, offices, citizens, and the state itself, which cannot subsist when only composed of bastards? But, it will be said, men will appeal as against abuses; they will summon, issue decrees, and seize on the temporalities. What a pity! The clergy, however little they may have, I do not say of courage, but of good sense, will let this be done and go their way; they will quietly permit appealing, adjourning, decreeing, seizing, and will end by remaining masters. It is not, it seems to me, a great sacrifice to abandon a part, when one is sure of getting possession of the whole.

CHAPTER 9

Conclusion

After laying down the principles of political right and attempting to establish the state on its foundations, it would remain to strengthen it in its external relations; which would comprise the law of nations, commerce, the right of war and conquests, public rights, alliances, negotiations, treaties, etc. But all this forms a new subject too vast for my limited scope. I ought always to have confined myself to a narrower sphere.